WORK TOWARD KNOWING:
BEGINNING WITH

BLAKE

WORK TOWARD KNOWING:
BEGINNING WITH

BLAKE

JIM WATT

*Eliza, Thanks
for Singing!
Jim Watt
4/21/16*

KINCHAFOONEE
CREEK PRESS ≈ ATHENS, GA

LIBRARY OF CONGRESS CATALOGING-IN-PUBLICATION DATA

Watt, Jim.
Work Toward Knowing: Beginning With Blake

ISBN: 978-1-312-99040-1

www.facebook.com/kinchpress

Printed in the United States of America on acid-free paper

Edited and designed by Norman Minnick

Contents

Illustrations

I have included these works to suggest the beauty of the individual voices of the Builders of Jerusalem; evidence of formal training in art are here subsumed by traces of the Four Zoas.

– J.W.

These and other images from the Blake seminars can be found in full-color and with commentary at beginningwithblake.wordpress.com.

Foreword: The Building of Jerusalem

One sunny day in April I was walking with Jim Watt and Doug von Koss along a path under fragrant Bradford Pear trees toward Jordan Hall where Jim's office was located on the campus of Butler University. Doug was a guest singer from San Francisco, invited to lead the students of Jim's Blake seminar in song. We stopped at the entrance as Doug read the inscription in the limestone above the door: ENTER TO LEARN • DEPART TO FULFILL. Jim was stunned, "Doug, I've been entering through this doorway for 35 years and have never noticed that before!" He was doing just that every day of those 35 years – learning and fulfilling.

*   *   *

My cubicle was situated just outside Jim's office. I learned more by eavesdropping on his conversations with students than I ever had in graduate or undergraduate studies. I was inspired by the music he would play at a high volume, disregarding his colleagues in neighboring offices, ranging from the blues of Howlin' Wolf or Muddy Waters to the classical piano of Maurizio Pollini or Hélène Grimaud to fado sung by Mariza. Sometimes he and a couple students who had come by to inquire about their grades would get carried away by impromptu singing, but because this was a highbrow academic institution, they drew no audience except my secretly listening ears.

*   *   *

Built in 1928, The Arthur Jordan Memorial Hall, designed in the Collegiate Gothic style by Robert Frost Daggett and Thomas Hibben, sits heavily on Butler University's campus with daunting buttresses, recessed entrances framed by pointed arches surrounded by stone moldings and intricate relief sculpture. Unlike the gothic cathedrals, though, Jordan Hall did not have expansive windows. With the exception of the president's office, which was lined with high, broad windows that allowed sunlight to flood the room all hours of the day, Jordan was the dankest building on campus.

*   *   *

Gothic architecture, the Gothic cathedral especially, represents the universe in microcosm. One of Blake's most well-known stanzas is this one from "Auguries of Innocence":

> To see a World in a Grain of Sand,
> And a Heaven in a Wild Flower,
> Hold Infinity in the palm of your hand,
> And Eternity in an hour

Blake says, "Gothic is Living Form...Living Form is Eternal Existence." Jim also taught courses on the Gothic cathedral.

*   *   *

With the exception of the occasional guest poet or loudmouthed student, Jim's classroom was the only one that buzzed with vibrant energy and light. He and his students were building Jerusalem. What does that mean? Anyone casually familiar with the Bible would say that Jerusalem is a metaphor for Heaven or a place of universal love and peace. But Blake's idea of the building of Jerusalem is probably more true to what genuine artists such as Jim Watt are doing because it does not discount our life on earth and in our bodies, leaving us yearning for some place beyond. Morris Eaves, in *A Blake Dictionary*, writes: "Jerusalem is the 'Divine Vision' in every individual." In *The Four Zoas*, Blake's longest poem, Urizen conspires with Luvah to enslave Liberty. Urizen represents rationality and Luvah represents emotion. And this is what happens to most of us when these two conflicting characteristics are the only attributes by which we experience reality. This is what our parents, teachers, priests, politicians, etc. have taught us. It is what Blake calls "Single Vision."

* * *

In *The Four Zoas*, the primal man, Albion, represents Man before the Fall, and each of us in a state of sleep or unawakened consciousness. In such a state the four fundamental aspects of man have been thrown off balance. These are represented in Blake's cosmology by the Four Zoas: Urizen (rationality) and Luvah (emotion), as mentioned above, but also Tharmas (sensation) and Urthona (intuition or imagination). "Though they are present in each of us," Watt explains, "they are also uniquely and individually unbalanced – and a considerable effort is required to bring them into balance." He continues, "The Zoas...will assist us in that recovery and recreation of one another and reality which Blake calls the building of Jerusalem."

* * *

As a poet with a particular fondness for the Romantics – Keats, Shelley, Byron, Wordsworth, Goethe, Hölderlin, Novalis, et al. – I knew a little Blake, but always found him difficult to comprehend. I tried to learn from academics such as Northrop Frye and Harold Bloom, but they were not speaking the same language as I. Robert Bly's *News of the Universe* provided a great introduction, but it wasn't until I saw in person some of Blake's prints and drawings from the *Book of Job* at the Indianapolis Museum of Art and in that same gallery attended what was supposed to be a lecture on Blake by Dr. James T. Watt, Allegra Stewart Professor of English at Butler University, that I was inspired to jump in, to begin with Blake. It wasn't long before Watt had everyone in attendance standing and singing verses of Blake! Watt explains in this

book, "...the words are not the meaning; the text is not the poem....
Actual experience...will confirm that the song is more than the notes...
and your own life is much more than material cause and effect. You
were not reasoned into being," he continues, "ask your parents. You
were thought, dreamed, imagined, sung and danced together into being." Later he shares a passage from *Jerusalem:*

> A mans worst enemies are those
> Of his own house & family;
> And he who makes his law a curse,
> By his own law shall surely die.
>
> In my Exchanges every Land
> Shall walk, & mine in every Land,
> Mutual shall build Jerusalem:
> Both heart in heart & hand in hand.

Watt asks, "How could we have anything to do with such building? Even
if we thought some action might be taken, what would it have to do
with art?" He responds, "Blake's art...is obviously and remarkably different from what we have been taught to expect of art. Specifically, it
makes powerfully spiritual, mental, emotional, and corporeal, or sensational demands on its audience."

*   *   *

The book you hold in your hands in more than a text on Blake. And
although its subtitle is *Beginning with Blake,* it is not only for beginners.
Besides being a guide to the work of William Blake, *Work toward Knowing*
is a vade mecum of sorts on teaching and learning and achieving fourfold vision. It is also a memoir of a man who understands Blake and
teaching and who is a master craftsman in the building of Jerusalem.
Enter this book to learn. Depart to fulfill.

Norman Minnick
Indianapolis, Indiana

The mind is its own place,

and in itself

Can make a Heaven of H-ll,

a Hell of Heaven.

The mind

Can make a

The mind is its own place,

and in itself

Can make a Heaven of H-ll,

a Hell of Heaven.

Prelude: A Golden String

In futurity
I prophetic see,
That the earth from sleep,
(Grave the sentence deep)

Shall arise and seek
For her maker meek:
And the desart wild
Become a garden mild.

WILLIAM BLAKE, "The Little Girl Lost"

It was an ordinary evening, a moon perhaps, a few clouds, but no threat of rain, no wind howling or even sighing. The house was not in the least unusual: a split-level, ranch style, set amongst others in the suburbs. The prior owner had died in it, but there was nothing in the least remarkable about her passing. Nor on the evening in question was I reading anything of a spiritual or occult nature; I was simply browsing through the *New York Times Book Review* when, about ten in the evening, I decided to get myself a snack. My wife was reading quietly alongside me. I asked her whether she wanted anything downstairs; she smiled, said a soft "no," and returned to her book.

When I went down the stairs, as I had hundreds of times before and have hundreds of times since, there was nothing noteworthy in the air. It was neither perfectly silent, nor unusually noisy: a car sped past, the lights flashing briefly on the walls, the furnace clicked on or off, and the house made its normal, settling-down-to-night-time noises. I switched on the kitchen lights and opened the refrigerator. I took out the chilled white wine and cheese and then got down some crackers. Then, while I was arranging the cheese slices on a plate, I knew that someone was in the living room, watching me.

Every now and then, when I'm in the library or waiting for a plane, reading or idly waiting for the appointed time to arrive, I have that feeling – and when I look up and around I'll find someone's eyes resting on me. The person will either smile, or make his or her eyes glaze over, or be startled and look away. The tension, the energy or force of their gaze will disappear as quickly as that.

This time, though, there was no one there to catch sight of. There was no one standing in the darkened doorway to the dining room, nor in the hall. In the kitchen window, I caught only the reflected image of an ordinary man in his bathrobe, his hand frozen above a plate of crackers and cheese with a somewhat sheepish look on his face. A look, not so much of fear as of confusion.

We all wonder what it would be like to intercept a burglar and I, like every other suburban male, have once or twice picked up a baseball bat or tennis racquet and set forth noisily down the stairs, turning on every light in the house and hoping to scare the source of some unusual sound back out the way it came in. At times like these I have remembered the stories of people being shot by intruders – my heart has been pumping and my senses strained to the slightest sound or movement. This time, though, I felt no fear, only puzzlement as to who was watching me – along with absolute certainty that she was there.

I was as sure the eyes were a girl's as I was aware of their presence. But on what basis? I was awake, I was thinking very clearly; clearly enough to wonder if I has hallucinating or going crazy. How could there be a girl in my living room at 10 o'clock at night? And why? (Oddly, I didn't ask myself how it was possible for her to watch me through the walls, but then nothing about this experience seemed to follow normal rules.) I put the plate down, walked past the refrigerator into the hall, turned right, and stepped into the living room. In front of me was the sofa and the large picture window. Once again, I could see my reflected image, the kitchen light behind me clearly outlining my form, my arm reaching out and my hand resting on the light switch.

I didn't switch on the lights; I didn't have to. I could see her about five feet to my right, standing beside the long table next to the book-case. She was about six or seven years old, in a nightdress and hold-ing – something – wrapped in a blanket or cloth under one arm. She was looking right at me. And she was crying. In fact, she seemed quite frightened. When I moved she jumped back and almost disappeared. So, naturally, I froze. Nor did I look directly at her because, when I did so, she faded somehow. I could only see her out of the corner of my eye, with my peripheral vision. I was surprised, then, to hear my own voice, speaking ever so softly and saying, "It's all right. Don't be frightened. I won't hurt you. It's OK; It's OK."

I hadn't the foggiest notion what was going on; but I knew that it would be OK if I just didn't scare her. So I stood there for a few mo-ments, making soothing noises and trying to get her to talk. It was evident that she expected me to throw her out and that I was not to get any closer than I already was. She had stopped crying at least. After a few moments, I thought, rather crazily, that I had better tell my wife what was going on or else she might be worried. But if I yelled upstairs I was afraid I'd scare the girl away – and probably my wife as well. So I said, Just a minute; I'll be right back.

I went up the stairs – and back into the normal world. My wife was just as I had left her: quietly reading in a pool of light, a pile of pillows behind her and the bedclothes bunched up over her knees. She looked up.

What are you doing? You look funny.

Well…there's a ghost in the living room.

What!? Her eyes widened.

No. No. I don't mean a bad ghost; just a little girl ghost.

Don't do this.

No. Really. Come and see for yourself.

This is not funny.

I'm not joking. There's this little girl, a ghost I guess, down in the living room. I think she's lost or something. Come and see.

I'm not going anywhere.

Come on. We've got to go down. She seems scared.

She's scared!

It's all right; she won't hurt us.

By this point I was sure I was having one of the best dreams I'd ever had. I didn't want to wake up though; I wanted to go back downstairs and have my little girl ghost reveal to me the secret hiding place of some vast fortune or something. So I got quite cheerful and giddy.

OK, if you won't come down – just a minute – I'll bring her up here.

And so I went back down the stairs. She was still there, maybe a little closer to the hall, maybe a little fainter – and maybe a little less frightened.

What do you want? I asked, wondering if ghosts always had to tell the truth. My wife's voice came down from the upstairs hall:

Are you all right? What's going on?

I'm fine; she's still here – but I don't think she's scared anymore.

It was clear to me that she wasn't going to talk to me – maybe she didn't understand English – so I just sort of stood there for a few minutes, making the kind of soothing noises you make for sick kids and puppies and wondering why I didn't feel like an absolute fool. And, after a time, she was gone. I felt her little spirit leave the same way I had felt it arrive: not violently or noisily or in a hurry and certainly not with any spite or malice, more like the way you feel the birds come and go in the trees. I guess I got her calmed down enough to find her way. I hope so.

When I turned on the light, there was my perfectly ordinary living room in my perfectly ordinary house. No ribbons fluttered down as in "Young Goodman Brown," her little bundle wasn't sitting on a chair, and back in the kitchen no cheese or crackers were missing from my plate. There was absolutely nothing out of the ordinary. So I picked up my snack, went back to the hall, turned off the kitchen and living room lights and went back up the stairs.

She's gone, I said. After a little interrogation in which I repeated most of what I've recounted here, I took a sip of wine, opened my review and read a few more pages. When I had finished the wine and cheese, I turned off my reading lamp, said goodnight – and slept as ordinarily as ever in my life. I must have dreamed – we always dream – but on waking I had no recollection of any further communication with my little girl lost. But everything was – and still is – as clear to me as any other thing in my memory.

I know that such reports are associated with unreliability and mental instability, with "New Agers," charlatans and those credulous folks who purchase supermarket tabloids to keep abreast of alien abduction schemes and Elvis sightings. And they also feature in the highly developed imaginative powers of certain contemporary writers, "magical realists" and the like. But I'm not crazy and I'm not trying to sell you anything, nor do I think I've been "given the key" – if I have, I haven't the dimmest notion of what it unlocks. And though I would characterize my approach to teaching (and to a lesser extent, to life) as intuitive, I always try to make my arguments as rational as possible. So what has this little narrative to do with teaching the illuminated books of William Blake? I hope that will become clearer as you read what follows. But to begin, I'd like to remind you that Blake, though highly imaginative, was himself no magical realist. Neither was he a charlatan or a credulous person – though many still dismiss him with those labels.

Blake spent his life telling everyone who would listen to him that the world we find ourselves in is infinitely more complex than the language(s) we use to describe it. Indeed, its limits and principles far exceed the rules of *any* language. He understood at least as well as Heisenberg, (and on far more immediate evidence), that reality mocks our efforts to describe it and that meaning itself evaporates under the pressure of our presumptive questioning. Still, he spent his life attempting to bring a simple and fundamental message to his fellow humans in the plainest possible language: "Mark well my words! they are of your eternal salvation."[1]

So what prevents us from hearing him? Is it the current, (i.e. nonsense) status of Religion? His aesthetic limitations? Though these have been offered in various ways by various readers and critics, I believe the cause is something much more pervasive, something shared across the entire spectrum of modern life and political, philosophical, scientific and religious thought. What gets in our way of hearing Blake is nothing less than the triumph of the scientific rationalism he so detested. I don't mean the scientific method; I don't mean the rise of technology; and I certainly don't mean empiricism, for all Blake ever asks is that you try – and try again. But scientific rationalism permits only certain kinds of trying; others are dismissed out of hand. Whatever is unique, concrete, particular and incommensurable – in a word, whatever is invaluable – is supposed by scientific rationalism to be either non-existent in "reality," or a distraction from it. And a man who insists, as Blake did, that the earth is flat and that he can touch the sky at the end of the street will definitely be perceived by the scientific rationalist as out of touch with reality and demanding a return to the superstition of the "Dark Ages." But what Blake objects to in the scientific rationalist's picture is its reductionism. For him, the parameters of time/space, so dear to the followers of Newton, are neither the conditions for, nor a description of, reality; they are the consequences of perception: "For the Eye altering alters all / The Senses roll themselves in fear / And the flat Earth becomes a Ball // The Stars Sun Moon all shrink away/ [leaving] A desart vast..."[2] Henry Crabb Robinson remembers Blake saying, "I do not believe the world is round. I believe it is quite flat." Robinson objected that it must be round since it had been circumnavigated (as a rationalist, today, would point to pictures from space). He then closes his account of the conversation with deliciously unconscious irony: "We were called to dinner at the moment and I lost the reply – "[3]

Blake's answer, not that Robinson could have grasped it, is clearly spelled out in *Milton:*

> The sky is an immortal Tent built by the Sons of Los
> And every Space that a Man views around his dwelling-place:
> Standing on his own roof, or in his garden on a mount
> Of twenty-five cubits in height, such space is his Universe;
> And on its verge the Sun rises & sets. the Clouds bow
> To meet the flat Earth...[4]

It is evident that Blake is fully cognizant of the circumnavigated earth so dear to Robinson and the rationalists; it is also clear that he pities its coldness and emptiness. The "Little Girl Lost" is exactly here, in the desart of the rationalists; she is the sleeping earth who, on waking and seeking her maker, will transform the "desart wild" into a "garden mild."[5] It is this vast, empty sky, so different from the tent of

Los, that Blake dismisses out of hand. Samuel Palmer's reminiscence of his impatience with scientific materialists is pertinent: "Being irritated by the exclusively scientific talk at a friend's house, which talk had turned on the vastness of space, he cried out, 'It is false. I walked the other evening to the end of the earth, and touched the sky with my finger.'"[6] The same tent of Los, the beautiful and ever changing sky waits at the end of your garden; you may touch it, if you wish, yourself. And, happily, it is not the case that you must go crazy, or see visions and dream dreams to appreciate William Blake. Nor must you be visited by ghosts. But you must be calm, pay attention, and stay sane – especially stay sane.

Blake was [and is] eminently sane. He may, indeed, have been the sanest man of the European Enlightenment. He thought every bit as carefully as Locke or Newton; though his premises and methods were strikingly different, his reasoning is just as consistent – and even more compelling. Only pay attention, he said, and you'll notice that whatever you know involves your senses as well as your reasoning capacity, touches and is touched by your feelings (or emotions) and your imagination (or intuition).[7]

Hearing and understanding Blake, then, depends on two things: first, on your listening with your whole (and balanced) being, and second, on your recognition that reality and the truth about it comes through the various attributes of your being, but is, itself, not of them. Though this is simply stated, it takes considerable effort (at first) to put it into practice. Indeed, one way of 'understanding' Blake's work may be to see it as a continual and multi-layered process of teaching us how to see and listen – and what to look and listen for.

My purpose here, however, is not to attempt an explanation of Blake's epistemology and ontology (this may not be possible). I simply hope to suggest a means of approaching his art, derived from his description of our actual relation to the world. An early and succinct statement of it may be found in some lines of a poem, "The Everlasting Gospel," he squeezed into the margins of his notebook:

> This Lifes dim Windows of the Soul
> Distorts the Heavens from Pole to Pole

And leads you to Believe a Lie
When you see with not thro the Eye.[8]

In this life, that is, the "Windows of the Soul" (not merely your eyes, but all your senses, as well as your reasoning capacity, feelings and intuition), distort reality when they make themselves the measure of the heavens. Blake understood the reason for this distortion (seeing "with" not "through") to be contained in the myth of the Fall, but he was not one to get bogged down in theological argument.[9] More importantly, his point is that though the means by which we process our experience are liable to distort it, it is not this distortion which is the problem; it is our belief that this distortion is all there is – or can be. For when you attempt to understand reality or truth with your powers rather than through them you are led, always and inevitably, back to yourself.[10] The consequence for art is exhaustion; for the individual, depression; and for society, war: "Art Degraded Imagination Denied War Governed the Nations"[11]

And you might well ask, at this point, what truth or reality can there be in this life, where we have learned to our lasting dismay that we can never escape our own subjectivity? Blake replies that reality and the truth are always and immediately accessible, 'in Eternity.' The seeing through to them is the end of his art. But, at the same time, vision, as he supremely shows, is not exercised in isolation: even the solo dancer is partnered by the dance. The notion of a self-sufficient truth, like any claim of self-sufficiency, cannot be trusted. "I have always found," he writes, "that Angels have the vanity to speak of themselves as the only wise; this they do with a confident insolence sprouting from systematic reasoning."[12]

It is this same "systematic reasoning" which is forever busily proposing either the reconstruction of the world after its theoretical model or dismissing it altogether and urging us to move as speedily as possible from it to the perfection of heaven. And while reasoning claims to honor originality and purports to be the sole source of truth, it is itself wholly unoriginal and its grasp of truth is both tentative and incomplete. Systematic reasoning, not surprisingly, disallows truth to poetry on the grounds that it lacks rigor and precision. And when systematic reasoning is made a basis of religious belief, it solemnly proposes that nature herself was only brought into existence by the word or law of a perfectly reasonable God as a means of manifesting (imperfectly) his creative powers. This God has several names and manifestations. Blake mostly calls him "Urizen," sometimes Satan, and once, "Nobodaddy." While reasoning is an enduring and necessary part of each of us, Blake asserts that when it is worshipped it turns tyrannical and manifests itself as a jealous, unforgiving Father God, the most familiar example being Jehovah in the Old Testament. Though today we are more likely to worship systematic reasoning in the sciences than the churches, the claim (that all reality is derived from reason and that to its judgment there is no appeal) remains the same. The voice of systematic reasoning is not one likely to comfort a little girl lost in the dark; it is even less likely to notice her.

Yet a lost little girl came to my house one quiet evening, and, having evidently found what she required, went on her way – leaving to me the problem of what to do with this part of my experience. For Urizen the solution is easy (or at least, automatic) enough: what cannot be incorporated in his world, that is the inexplicable, is denied. Regrettably, he says, joined with his partner, Morality, this imperfect world we live in persists in presenting us with less than satisfactory experience. Blake's response brushes aside reason's doubts and morality's hesitations in the face of this life: "I know of no other Christianity and of no other Gospel," he writes in *Jerusalem*, "than the liberty both of body & mind to exercise the Divine Arts of Imagination." On the same page is the following quatrain:

> I give you the end of a golden string,
>> Only wind it into a ball:
> It will lead you in at Heavens gate,
>> Built in Jerusalems wall.[13]

So what if Blake's right? What if there's nothing fundamentally wrong with the world and that finding out how to live *in* it requires us to do no more than pay attention *to* it? Whether this be true of the world and your experience of it, only you can say. But it certainly is true about Blake's art that there is nothing wrong with it, if you pay attention to it. But "paying attention" means here nothing less than seeing through the windows of your soul, not with them. Thus Blake's prayer for us all:

> Now I a fourfold vision see
> And a fourfold vision is given to me
> Tis fourfold in my supreme delight
> And three fold in soft Beulahs night
> And twofold Always. May God us keep
> From Single vision & Newtons sleep[14]

Amen.

This little book is my part in a joint effort to assist us in rising, in our supreme delight, to four fold vision – and to prevent our falling back to Newton's sleep. Your part consists in surrendering some of your ordinary presumptions about significance (that it is a matter of logic and data, for instance), and attempting a kind of reading which requires rather more discipline and attention to detail than you have been accustomed to employ. Finding the golden string and winding it are not activities for either passive listeners or skeptics; what we do, we have to do together. But the results of both the finding and the winding will speak for themselves. And if you think you know, right now, what to expect, I understand: I was sure I knew, too. After all, if there really is a golden string, how hard can it be to find?

Years ago, at the University of North Carolina at Chapel Hill in the Sixties, I was one of the lucky graduate students who collected around the leadership of O.B. Hardison, Jr., brilliant teacher, scholar and author of several remarkable books. We took all the courses from him we could and after class, we followed him from the lectern, down the hall to his office, and even over to his rambling house near the campus. He was always spinning out ideas – his own, those of his friends and colleagues, and, most excitingly of all, ours. He would listen to a question or remark, extract the idea that lay beneath it, put a couple of twists in it and hand it back with suggestions as to where the answer might be found.

One afternoon at his house – I think we were out by the swimming pool, for I seem to remember O.B.'s face wet and dripping – I brought up Blake's *Milton*. I was then laying plans for a dissertation on *Paradise Lost*. My remarks that afternoon had to do with my disappointment with Blake's poem. I had run across a reference to Blake's "inversion" or "reversal" of *Paradise Lost* and, as my studies were then focused on the structural details of the epic in general and Milton in particular, I had turned to Blake's poem for some instruction.

All who remember their first reading of *Milton*, can appreciate my dismay. After struggling through several pages of text (and a couple of partial, and badly printed, photo reproductions), I returned to the sane and logical structure of *Paradise Lost* (and "reality") with relief. I may have even muttered to myself what a cruel jest it was for Fate to rob Milton of his sight while letting Blake put it to such a chaotic use. Anyway, what I think I said that afternoon to O.B. was that Blake may have been right when he identified Milton as "a true Poet," and that he may have even been correct when he said he was "of the Devil's party," but to say that he was so "without knowing it," was the height of presumption on the part of someone who himself knew nothing about epic poetry.

Oh, said O.B. innocently, Blake knew nothing about epic?

Well, I replied, eager to show off, He certainly set out to "correct" *Paradise Lost,* the Preface to *Milton* states that clearly enough, but isn't it equally clear that he failed? For instance, he seems to begin in medias res, all right – but he never gets anywhere! Pretty soon the thing falls completely apart; it's not so much a reversal of Milton as it is a mess.

'In medias mess,' offered another student. But O.B. ignored him.

The real question, he said, is why he makes it so obvious. Maybe, if you took the thing apart, you'd find an answer.

This remark struck me with such force that I decided, then and there, to do a Master's Thesis on *Milton*. Ever the obedient student, I took the poem apart. I even did a pretty fair job of arguing in my thesis that it is, in fact, a reversal of *Paradise Lost,* one which (unsuccessfully) incorporates the details of Milton's and Blake's biographies and psychologies into a personal mythological system. It was duly approved and filed in the library. I filed it away, too.

I was disappointed with my argument, frustrated by a sense of never having actually touched the poem, but I assumed my disappointment was just a part of the learning process. Of course, that wasn't the real reason, nor was it the fault of my long-suffering and patient director, Robert Kirkpatrick; (long-suffering because he loved Blake and patient because I was determined to make Blake "make sense"). I went on, with relief, to my dissertation project with Jerry Mills, which focused on a series of tropes in the epic from Homer to Milton. I proved, to Jerry's and my committee's satisfaction, that such poems were carefully structured by their poets to clarify for each audience member his role in the construction and preservation of society. The epic required, as I saw it, an architectural logic, a reasoned structure, otherwise it would collapse under its own weight. I was still really arguing with Blake – though at the time, I would have denied it. And the more I argued, the less satisfied I was with my argument. So I did what most people busy proving themselves right do: I turned my attention to other things. And there were plenty: I was busy teaching (or learning how not to) and starting a family. Time, as it will, passed.

I taught the courses expected of English faculty in a small, private university: freshman comp., sophomore genre courses, occasionally a Late Renaissance, or a Milton course. Never Blake. Then, one semester, I offered a seminar in the metaphor of the Eucharist in English poetry. I needed to move, somehow, from George Herbert to Gerard Hopkins and I thought Blake might make a useful contrast – and maybe even a bridge. Something quite unexpected happened, though: both the students and I found Blake's insistence on the holiness of the body more compelling (both poetically and spiritually) than the more doctrinally correct poets' meditations on the mystery of the Eucharist. When one of my students wanted to dip into *Milton* for his term paper, wondering if the poet's descent from Eternity to Felpham mightn't be a Eucharistic parallel or parody, whose laughter was it I heard echoing in the back corridors of my mind: Hardison's? Blake's?

At any rate, having dipped my toes again into the stream of Blake's music, I somehow decided (or it was decided for me?) to really take the plunge. One day, I heard myself, to my amazement, proposing a seminar on Blake's Prophetic Books.

You don't mean those crazy ones, do you? said my department head.

Yes, I said, trying to sound as casual as possible, I'll do the *Songs*, of course, and the *Marriage*, but I want to focus on the prophecies:

Thel, Los, America, Europe, Urizen. Definitely *Milton*. I don't know about *Jerusalem*. There may not be time for it.

No, she said, I imagine not.

But she approved it. After all, it was, as she observed, my idea.

That summer, I read through Blake. And I felt a little uneasy. I read the main critical works: Frye, naturally, Bloom, and Erdman. I read Jean Hagstrum's *William Blake, Poet and Painter* and W.J.T. Mitchell's *Blake's Composite Art*. I felt more uneasy. Something familiar was happening: the more I read, the less I could see a way of actually teaching Blake. I could assign the readings, and I could "cover" them in class, but how could I make my students feel connected to their bewilderingly personal mixture of music and myth? It was my master's thesis all over again: I had plenty of answers, but they didn't seem to be connected to Blake. It was like the time I tried to teach the *Tao Te Ching* in spite of the fact that Lao Tsu makes it perfectly clear that the Tao that can be taught is not the Tao. I was up against the irreducible fact that William Blake devoted the main portion of his life to the creation of works that no one read. Or reads. And the problem, it appears, does not lie with the readers.

Take, for instance, Modernist texts like Joyce's *Ulysses* or Faulkner's *The Sound and the Fury*. These were found difficult even by sophisticated readers when they were first published, but they are grasped readily enough today by undergraduate English majors. Blake's prophetic books, on the other hand, continue to baffle even specialists. As one scholar wrote, "Modern criticism has only begun the task of defining, much less elucidating Blake's text, especially the visual-verbal text of his unique illuminated books. And the taste for Blake's work in our time is grounded in such widely diverse and often contradictory values that it must be subject to some degree of correction or we are faced with a hopeless muddle."[15] If there's a golden string, it isn't leaping off the page.

No wonder, then, that as the summer came to an end, my syllabus was still little more than a reading list. The course description was in the class schedule; the books were in the bookstore, the class was filling up with students – and I had no idea what I was going to do with them. As the first day drew ever nearer, I did the only thing I could do: I gave up worrying. Then, I remembered a "remaindered" book I had picked up on sale – and never really looked at. Returning to Jim Bogan and Fred Goss's wild and wonderful book, *Sparks of Fire: Blake in a New Age,*[16] I came upon Morris Eaves' excellent essay, "Teaching Blake's Relief Etching,"[17] which takes a "hands on" approach to Blake's art by assigning students the task of creating a linoleum block print.

I could hardly contain my excitement; this had to be the way in I was looking for. Introducing my students to a similar process to that by which the Illuminated books came into being, I would be able to focus their attention, physically, on the windows of their souls and how these combine to create their signature imaginations, those particular manifestations in this world of time and space of the "Imagination or the Divine Body in Every Man."[18] By assigning them the task of "illuminating" a text, I would be providing them with an experiential basis for understanding how word and design combine to make meaning both individual – in the most minute particulars – and transcendent. My lack of just such experiential knowledge, I decided, must have been the reason I had such a difficult time reading Blake's *Milton* all those years before. In the first place, I hadn't read what Blake actually engraved; I read a transcript – full of editorial intervention and set up in type – of the text of *Milton* and I dealt in only a very limited sense with the relation of Blake's words to his designs. Yet another bonus occurred to me: that in the carving of a block text and design, they would get a tangible experience of reversal, a vital part of Blake's vision. For not only did he, as an engraver, constantly work with reversal in design and text, in ground and line, in light and dark, but a substantial portion of his thought involves reversing our commonly accepted categories: "...thou readst black," he writes, "where I read white."[19]

So I ordered the linoleum blocks, cutting tools and water color sets and completed the syllabus. I had found the "golden string" for my students, now all they had to do was wind it into a ball to be led in at "Heaven's gate." They would be creating their own designs and, by their individual lights, would, somehow, find their way. At least, that was what I hoped. Then, two days before the first meeting, I picked up the class roster and discovered that one of my students was – blind! Because I was only beginning with Blake, I thought this was nothing more than an unfortunate accident, something I'd have to work around rather than through.

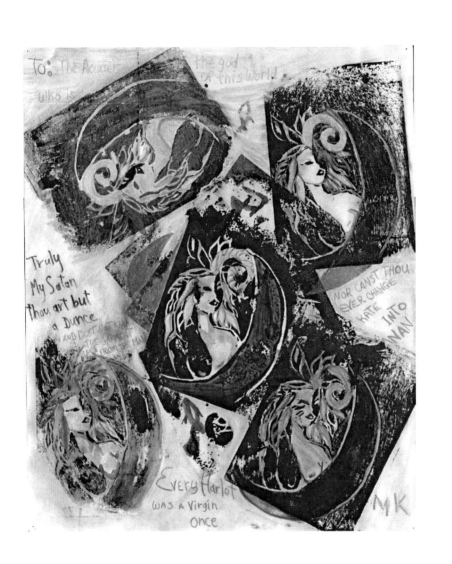

To: The Accuser the god of this World!
Who is

Truly
My Satan
Thou art but
a Dunce
AND DOST NOT KNOW
THE GARMENT
FROM THE MAN

NOR CANST THOU
EVER CHANGE
KATE
INTO
MAN

Every Harlot
WAS a Virgin
once

MK

One: Beginning with Blake

And their words seemed to them as idle tales, and they
believed them not.

LUKE 24:11

After the Crucifixion, two of the disciples set
out for a place called Emmaus on some business. They were intimates
of Jesus, people who had spent months with him, if not years. And
they were witnesses to the events surrounding his trial and execution.
As they talked and reasoned about what they had seen and heard, a
man joined them. They were surprised that he hadn't heard about
Jesus. Indeed, they said, they themselves had even believed him to
be the Messiah, "he which should have redeemed Israel." And, they
added, according to the testimony of some women, he had risen from
the dead; they had seen him, or a vision of him. But when others went
they found only the empty tomb.

Luke makes it clear from the beginning that the man who walked
and talked with the two disciples was, in fact – and in the physical
body – Jesus; he was not an hallucination, nor was he disguised. But
the two disciples didn't recognize him. When they finished telling him
all that they knew, he berated them for doubting what the women had
reported. Then, beginning with the Pentateuch, he explained all that
is to be found in the scriptures concerning himself. They still didn't

recognize him. As they approached Emmaus and it appeared that he was going on without them, they invited him to have dinner with them. While they were eating, he blessed some bread and gave it to them – and "their eyes were opened, and they knew him; and he vanished out of their sight."[1]

We think we know what is real and we think we know its limits. We doubt reports of transgressions of those limits; we even doubt our own experiences outside them. We think we have no choice; for we were all born alike and came to self-awareness in whatever circumstances history and our tribe contrived: and everything, ourselves included, that has a beginning must also have an end. Jesus died and was buried. But like Luke's story, Blake's designs and poems defy those limits – and to the same end. When we (think we) know what is before us, when we see it "with our own eyes" (not through them), we not only do not, we cannot, recognize it. Likewise, when our eyes are "opened," and we see through them, Jesus (or the stranger) is able to "vanish," being seen, now, in all things. But first we find ourselves on the road, going about our business and talking about our disappointment(s). For we, too, have believed. And would like still to believe. But the tomb is empty.

Is it not to forget about the empty tomb that we ask this stranger to have a meal and spend the evening with us? And then, just when we are caught up in that most fleeting of moments, with the taste of bread and wine on our tongues, do we not, inexplicably and suddenly, recognize him? But wait. Luke's story doesn't end in the moment of recognition. The two disciples return immediately to Jerusalem where they share what they have seen. And, in the sharing, once again they see, dine with, and handle Jesus. So may we. Matthew records these words: "Where two or three are gathered together in my name, there am I in the midst..." (Matt. 18:20). But, you say, the meaning of those words is (it must be) that Jesus is only spiritually (that is, symbolically) present. What happened to the disciples is unavailable to us, save metaphorically.

And how, asks Blake, do you know? What, or who, has told you that space/time, indeed reality itself, is simple – "One curse, one weight, one measure / One King, one God, one Law"?[2] Who, or what, has told you that the divine, or spiritual is abstract and available only to the reasoning mind or self? Is it not Urizen (Your Reason)? who argues that it is only in his ideal realm, divorced from the troublesome particulars of material, that is "actual" existence, that we may find that perfection and purity which are the prime attributes of the divine? But Blake will have none of this. And, neither, according to him, will Jesus. Henry Crabb Robinson, seeking to find assurances of this separation of the divine from the natural or human, asked Blake whether he believed in the divinity of Jesus. "He is the only God." Blake immediately responded, " – And so am I and so are you." A little later the poet also dismissed the notion of divine purity: "'Pure,' said Blake, 'do you think there is any purity in God's eyes – the angels in heaven are no more so than we.'"[3]

I have my students read Luke's post crucifixion narrative at the first meeting so that we may begin by considering this matter of seeing and believing: the way in which what we think we know blinds us to reality, and the way our hunger and thirst for the real opens our eyes. Knowing has been, for most of us, something we thought we collected and wielded (put in golden bowls and silver rods). But for Blake, knowing is a matter of surrender, of balance. Each step leads to the next, to hesitate is to fall, and every day begins with the stone rolled from the tomb.

> You dont believe I wont attempt to make ye
> You are asleep I wont attempt to wake ye
> Sleep on Sleep on while in your pleasant dreams
> Of Reason you may drink of Lifes clear streams
> Reason and Newton they are quite two things
> For so the Swallow & the Sparrow sings
> Reason says Miracle. Newton says Doubt
> Aye thats the way to make all Nature out
> Doubt Doubt & dont believe without experiment
> That is the very thing that Jesus meant
> When he said Only Believe Believe & try
> Try Try & never mind the Reason why[4]

This is Blake on the collision between what *his* reason told him (that all life is a miracle) and what his age considered "reasonable" (that the only access to nature is by systematic reduction of it to calculation and doubt). The story of the raising of Lazarus (John 11), is strikingly relevant to this little poem – and its closing words so casually attributed to Jesus. John's narrative opens with some interesting remarks about sleeping and on seeing and not seeing. The disciples are worried about Jesus returning to a place where the Jews had tried to stone him. He replies:

> Are there not twelve hours in the day? If any man walk in the day, he stumbleth not, because he seeth the light of the world.
> But if a man walk in the night, he stumbleth because there is no light in him.
> These things said he: and after that he saith unto them, Our friend Lazarus sleepeth; but I go, that I may awake him out of sleep. (John 11:9-11)

In his poem, Blake sets the raising of Lazarus against the empirical method. In twelve short lines, he compresses Jesus' strange remarks, Martha's passionate belief, Mary's doubts, and his own refusal to argue with those who cannot see because they will not ("...he groaned in the spirit and was troubled" John 11:33, & see also 38). For there is no arguing with doubt, since it puts out the light within and thus guarantees the doubter's stumbling (John 11:9-10).[5] Was it, Blake asks, doubt Jesus had in mind when he said to Mary: "I am the resurrection and the life: he that believeth in me, though he were dead, yet shall he live: And whosover liveth and believeth in me shall never die. Believest thou this?" (John 11:25-26)

Now before you throw down the book and leave the room, fearful that Blake is some kind of bible-thumping reactionary with glittering eyes, consider how neatly he has ignored the emphasis in John's version on the raising of Lazarus, and turned his attention, instead, to the matters of sleeping and waking, doubting and believing – and the application of these to the struggle between the enemies of faith, doubters who have reserved the use of reason to themselves exclusively, and those who still believe in the miracle of every day. Though those calling themselves agents of reason allow the existence of what they call "religious belief," they are quick to claim sole possession of universal validity for science's description of reality. And when that claim is challenged, their response is as deadly as it is swift. Blake understands, because he knew it in his life, why the raising of Lazarus, rather than converting them, convinced the chief priests and Pharisees to murder Jesus (John 11:46-53).

The pious hypocrisy of those who pretend to the status of priest and artist in order to preserve their own power always rouses Blake's indignation and sarcasm. In his defense of Thomas Paine and his attacks on Bishop Watson, in his fury with John Thornton, and in his disgust at the smug condescension of Joshua Reynolds, we find the same indignation, sarcasm, and barely concealed fury.[6] Paine is, for Blake, a believer, greater far than his opponent, who, for all his Bishop's robes, is as much a skeptic and doubter as Newton, Voltaire, Rousseau and the others Blake sees as enemies of truth and destroyers of Jerusalem. They are revealed in *Milton* in the figure of "the idiot Questioner," who,

> ...is always questioning,
> But never capable of answering, who sits with a sly grin,
> Silent, plotting when to question, like a thief in a cave;
> Who publishes doubt & calls it knowledge; whose Science is
>   Despair
> Whose pretence to knowledge is Envy, whose whole Science is
> To destroy the wisdom of the ages to gratify ravenous Envy
> That rages round him like a Wolf day & night without rest.
> He smiles with condescension; he talks of Benevolence &
>   Virtue
> (And those who act with Benevolence & Virtue, they murder
>   time on time!).
> These are the destroyers of Jerusalem; these are the murderers
> Of Jesus, who deny the Faith & mock at Eternal Life,
> Who pretend to Poetry that they may destroy Imagination
> By imitation of Nature's Images drawn from Remembrance.[7]

Against this hypocrisy and pretense which masks a murderous violence, Blake sets the ones who take Jesus at his word, the ones who will, "Believe Believe & try / Try Try & never mind the reason why." And who are these heroes? They must be, can be no other than – you and I. We, together, need to Try. Try. And Try – believing, not doubting. And what we need to believe is not dogma, and certainly not an interpretation sanctioned by those who are supposed to be wiser than we, including, especially, the teacher(s). This is very important. The work is both individual and cooperative, creative and non-hierarchical.

One of the *Songs of Innocence* begins with what seems to be a simple question:

> Little Lamb who made thee
> Dost thou know who made thee

We immediately assume that the speaker's question is directed not at the Lamb, but at us – and we leap to supply what we take to be the "right" answer: "God made the Lamb." Included in this leap is the notion that, of course, the Lamb is only a 'figure' of ignorance, a (simple) metaphor (the irony here, as always in Blake, is stinging!). It also ignores the striking stress in the second line on the word "know." For when you say, "Yes, I do know," your knowing stops at a word: God. And the rest of the poem becomes a familiar (and sentimental) Sunday School lesson. When, however, you reply, "No. I really don't know," you not only understand that you are the Lamb addressed, but you are ready to listen to the rest of the poem ("Little Lamb I'll tell thee!") and in that listening, to begin your work toward knowing.

Some remarks of Peter Brook on the twentieth century mystic, G.I. Gurdjieff's method may be pertinent here. Gurdjieff's work, says Brook, "was based on two things...One was always saying, Don't take this for granted, don't believe me, work this out for yourself – which is opposite to the common idea of a teacher. The other is that if you want to understand something beyond a certain point, you cannot do it alone."[8] 'Wait,' I hear you thinking, 'didn't you just establish doubt as the enemy? And now you're telling us to doubt you?!' No. I am saying that to try to find the answers we need, we have first to believe in our capacity to hear and see them *for ourselves* as opposed to being told and shown them. This struggle to really trust our individual perception requires the trying and trying again, the belief Blake sets against doubt. And as much as we have to believe in the process, we have, as well, *to share it* with one another. It is too much to expect any one to manage alone. Even Blake had his angels. The "proof" will be in the sharing, not its result or product, which – whether individual or joint – will always be no more than an approximation. For Jerusalem is, as we shall discover, always building, never finished.

You may join this on-going building process right now, by saying aloud: "I am of infinite value and eternal significance." Blake assumes this to be as true of you, and as natural as your breathing.[9] Look around while you are saying and trying to believe it; allow yourself to notice how different everything is, or would be, if it were true. Keep trying. If you find it too difficult to try; investigate the source of the difficulty in yourself. Locate, physically and emotionally, as well as intellectually where your struggle is actually located. The more real your resistance, the better. If you wish, take a moment to record your objections in detail; I'll return to the matter of opposition and resistance later. But for now let me go on to some further assumptions Blake makes about reality which you also need to "try on," both in your reading of Blake and in your own experience and existence. For it isn't enough, as you will soon discover, to tell yourself to remember that "Blake believed these things," and proceed with your reading and study. The considerable gap between your own notions of reality and those of Blake, in which his poetry has its origins and movement, if addressed only intellectually, will quickly result in considerable frustration and a severe blocking of your capacity to experience and/or enjoy Blake's art. Think of trying out these notions in your own life as a kind of "thought experiment;" no one, not Blake and certainly not me, is here to proselytize.

Blake also assumes that *everything is really and essentially connected.* All things and all persons are connected, both penetrating and being penetrated by, every other thing. When not blocked by will or fear, this flowing is joyous, as when Blake reports to us that, "...all this Vegetable World appeard on my left Foot, / As a bright sandal formd immortal of precious stones and gold: / I stooped down & bound it on to walk forward thro' Eternity."[10] But the reasoning ego, who is Urizen, finds continuity and interpenetration intolerable and vehemently denies it, not only holding itself apart, but insisting that apart-ness is the rule of existence: God/Man; Man/Woman; Self/other. Indeed, we find ourselves in a culture which has made the separate individual and power relations, or competition among individuals, the incontestable presupposition to all forms of thought and action. And our visual sense (the one most naturally associated with reasoning) appears to present us with separable objects, far and near, acting in space and time. Our languages, too, whether verbal or purely symbolic, as in mathematical functions, present us with a defined series of separable objects and functions. Over against these alienating hierarchical divisions, Blake sets that continuity and clarity which make the unity, instantly recognized and constantly sought, of art and truth. In lines reminiscent of the landscapes of Van Gogh and Cézanne, he asks,

> Can such an Eye judge of the stars? & looking thro its tubes
> Measure the sunny rays that point their spears on Udanadan;
> Can such an Ear filld with the vapours of the yawning pit,
> Judge of the pure melodious harp struck by a hand divine?
> Can such closed Nostrils feel a joy? or tell of autumn fruits
> When grapes & figs burst their covering to the joyful air?[11]

That energy, interpenetrating and uniting each created thing, even the grapes on the vine, contrasts sharply with Newton's mechanical universe of separate objects bouncing off one another like billiard balls.[12] For Blake, the cosmos is both filled with, and sustained by, divine energy, "For not one sparrow can suffer, & the whole Universe not suffer also, / In all its Regions, & its Father & Saviour not pity and weep."[13] This is possible because the universe is not made up of static and isolated entities, but consists in interpenetrating consciousnesses, each a tangent of multiple, and fluid, sources. Ernst Fenellosa illuminates this subtly by calling our attention to the difference between our fluid experience and the static language we use to describe it: "A true noun, an isolated thing [or person] does not exist in nature. Things are only the terminal points, or rather the meeting points, of actions, cross sections cut through actions, snapshots. Neither can a pure verb, an abstract motion, be possible in nature."[14]

    I remarked earlier that I would return to the resistance some of us have felt to the notion of our own eternal and infinite value. No doubt much of this dismissal of all but a relative value for oneself and for others is a consequence of a belief in one's individual isolation in a random system. For if we are no more than an accidental recombination of DNA and whatever environment chance assigns us, how could we have anything but relative value? Yet when we feel ourselves unjustly treated, we are quick to complain that those who mistreated us should have done otherwise! Yet, if their actions are merely the consequence of random energies, how can we label them just or unjust? Is it not because we immediately feel and cherish our own responsibility, thus we demand it of, not merely extend it to, others? This could, indeed, be explained as just another random phenomenon, a kind of illusion rising purely by chance in essentially un-free entities. But if the entire universe is essentially interconnected, and not a single sparrow can suffer without the whole universe suffering, then neither can one of us suffer alone and unnoticed. This is not to say that it can't seem to us that we are suffering alone. That itself is a large part in our suffering. And so is the mysterious sympathy we feel for those suffering around us. We are deeply involved in mystery here; something that surrounds us and reaches into our hearts:

> Why does the Raven cry aloud and no eye pities her?
> Why fall the Sparrow & the Robin in the foodless winter?
> Faint! shivering they sit on leafless bush, or frozen stone
>
> Wearied with seeking food across the snowy waste; the little
> Heart, cold; and the little tongue consum'd, that once in
>   thoughtless joy
> Gave songs of gratitude to waving corn fields round their
>   nest.[15]

It seems to the Raven that no eye pities her, but we are moved, not only by her suffering, but even by the recital of it. Why she suffers is a mystery, but that she suffers and that we pity her in this interconnected world is a fact. A corollary, then, of Blake's belief in the connectedness of all things, is his conviction that, in reality, *there are no accidents.*[16] Everything is divinely caused – a consequence of incommensurable agencies or forces – and has a meaning. Nothing "just happens."

And every Natural Effect has a Spiritual Cause, and Not

A Natural: for a Natural Cause only seems, it is a Delusion[17]

As Blake explains, the inter-connectedness and divine meaning of creation allows no opening for the random or the meaningless:

> God is in the lowest effects as well as in the highest causes;
> for he is become a worm that he may nourish the weak. For
> let it be rememberd that creation is God descending accord-
> ing to the weakness of man, for our Lord is the word of God
> & every thing on earth is the word of God & in its essence is
> God.[18]

Of course, we have abstractions like calendars and tables of the elements to help us organize our everyday life, even as we have languages to describe reality. But real water is not made up of two parts hydrogen and one part oxygen any more than real weather is as described by the calendar. Our theories, in fact, only function by ignoring the unimportant or insignificant things – like our lives and the starvation and fall of a sparrow.[19]

And if, indeed, there are no coincidences, then there is a reason – or a series of reasons – for my having thought about and written this sentence and a reason for your reading and thinking about it right now, in this particular moment.[20] Not yesterday and not tomorrow, but Now. And just as we are actually here, we are here for one another, and not least for those who scorn and deny us. Again, what we have to offer one another, the reason for our intersection, is a mystery. But that doesn't mean it doesn't exist. When I began my first Blake seminar, I thought I had to figure out some way of discouraging Jackie Miller, my blind student, from staying in the class because her blindness would make the work impossible for her. I thought, that is, that we had nothing to offer one another. Of course, she turned out to be an essential part of the class, more important, certainly, than the teacher. Though I can't say what she took from me, I can say that this book began with her.

Marguerite Yourcenar turned an interviewer's casual remark – 'Bread is made according to recipes.' – into an occasion for teaching us about reality and art:

Only a bad cook turns every five minutes to the cookbook. You have to vary things according to your mood, you have to adapt the recipe to the materials at hand. Bread is never made twice in the same way. And sometimes things go wrong. Winters here are very cold. It's hard to get the dough to rise without heating the kitchen as hot as an oven. You can never be sure that it will work. There are stages in bread-making quite similar to the stages in writing. You begin with some thing shapeless, which sticks to your fingers, a kind of paste. Gradually that paste becomes more and more firm. Then there comes a point when it turns rubbery. Finally you sense that the yeast has begun to do its work: the dough is alive. Then all you have to do is let it rest. But in the case of a book the work may take ten years.[21]

The recipe is where we begin, but the bread is never made twice the same way. So, too, the poem is never read twice the same way. We have to adapt it to the materials at hand. It is hot work and we can never be sure when the yeast has done its work and the bread, or poem, has come to life. But the work demands that we pay strict attention to the materials at hand – and adapt the recipe to them, not vice versa.

It isn't possible to separate Blake's art from his purpose: he is a prophet. And, like any prophet, he isn't particularly religious. Not for him Paul's grudging admission that, though prophecy and the spirit are to be preferred, they are to operate only in private. He doesn't require "silence in the churches." Nor does he insist, like the Saint, "that ye all speak the same thing, and that there be no divisions among you." Not for him are "...all things [to] be done decently and in or-der."[22] Instead, he takes as his motto Moses' wonderful rejoinder to Joshua: "would God that all the Lord's people were prophets."[23] And he means it, for he is a real – and reality – chef: he knows that whereas the recipe (or reason) brings together the materials, the cooking is the work of the spirit. He knows, further, that what is wanted at the table is inspired, not formula, food. The intellect, or the reasoning ego, is responsible both for the deadliness of institutions and the sadness of their diets, not because it is "reasonable," but because it, unreasonably, denies its origin:

> Refusing to behold the Divine image, which all behold
> And live thereby. he is sunk down into a deadly sleep
> But we immortal in our own strength, survive by stern debate
> Till we have drawn the Lamb of God into a mortal form
> And that he must be born is certain, for One must be All
> And comprehend within himself all things both small & great[24]

Refusal to behold. When we sacrifice the real to theory, to order and uniformity, whatever the reason, we are refusing to accept, or see the value in, that by which we all live. We are, then, indeed sunk in sleep.

Blake calls that which we refuse to behold, "the Divine Image;" Yourcenar calls it "the materials at hand" and you might call it simply, "the given." The tension between our actual experience and the various "recipes" for reality we have inherited means, for Blake, that *art and Christianity require us constantly to (re)construct the world.* Thus, for Blake, our function here is to assist one another in this great task by sharing our perceptions freely, that is, by openly and fully debating them. Sharing our perceptions is, however, not the same thing as arguing our prejudices. In order to share our perceptions, we must, first of all, be aware of them; in other words, we need to be awake, to pay attention.

The first step to paying attention in a classroom is not taking notes. Indeed, note-taking is a way of NOT paying attention. It discounts three fourths of what you are perceiving at any given time and thus reduces that reality to a series of abstractions and clichés.[25] When you are really paying attention, you see, you learn – and you don't forget. In fact, you *can't* forget, because learning is, properly understood, an effort of mind, body, heart and soul. Consequently what you are studying fundamentally changes who and where you are – how could you forget that?

Of course, "the powers that be," both inside and around us, oppose this kind of learning and this kind of change; Blake addresses the institutional opposition directly:

> All Bibles or sacred codes have been the causes of the follow-
>   ing Errors:
> 1. That Man has two existing principles Viz.: a Body & a Soul.

2. That Energy, calld Evil, is alone from the Body & that
   Reason, calld Good, is alone from the Soul.
3. That God will torment Man in Eternity for following his
   Energies.

But the following Contraries to theses are True:

1. Man has no Body distinct from his Soul for that calld Body
   is a portion of Soul discernd by the five Senses, the chief
   inlets of Soul in this age.
2. Energy is the only life and is from Body, and Reason is
   bound or outward circumference of Energy.
3. Energy is Eternal Delight.[26]

Sacred codes are today located less in the churches than in the universities. Although the language is slightly different, the essential hostility to energy and wholeness is still alive and well. For, though secular moderns have claimed to be materialists, the "material" they worship is actually a theory of matter, which they derive not from the soul (a word out of fashion) but from reason itself. The body, though, is still seen as the source of all our problems – and far from viewing energy as eternal delight, moderns worry that entropy, or the exhaustion of energy in a closed system, is the source of ultimate extinction: we die, the sun dies: everything dies: nothing matters.

Blake's art, in short, requires an inversion or reversal of most of our sacred codes: it assumes that value is absolute, not relative; that existence is continuous, not divided; that everything has meaning; nothing has been left to chance; and, finally, that our (communal) task as free agents is the on-going re-creation of this world. Of course, we can choose otherwise. And, for most of history, we have. Something both in- and out-side us opposes these beliefs and this task at every turn. The struggle, in all its varied forms and manifestations, between those who are building and those who tearing down Jerusalem is the principal theme of Blake's prophetic art. The resistance we feel to Blake's notion of our absolute value and eternal significance; our discomfort with the notion that "everything on earth is the word of God & in its essence is God;"[27] these are instances of the power of the destroyers of the Holy City. Blake identifies that opposition with Paul's famous warning: "For we wrestle not against flesh and blood, but against principalities, against powers, against the rulers of the darkness of this world, against spiritual wickedness in high places."[28]

Because Blake's art is devoted neither to our entertainment nor to our instruction, but to the defeat of "spiritual wickedness in high places," it makes extraordinary demands on us. That he is difficult both to read and to teach is a commonplace. Probably the most forthright presentation of the problem is F.R. Leavis':

> The question I have in mind, then, when I speak of Blake as a challenge may be thought of as this: what kind of approach should one make it one's aim to develop in working with students in a university English school? One certainly can't, if at all responsible, say 'Get the Blake in the Oxford Standard Authors and read it through', or 'Dip pertinaciously, sample copiously, and you'll soon begin to find your bearings, and before long have notes for the organized and really repaying study.' There isn't any book one can recommend as a guide... In fact, it is one's responsibility to warn the student against being hopeful of light and profit to be got from the Blake authorities and the Blake literature. More than that, he should be told, unequivocally that none of the elaborated prophetic works is a successful work of art.[29]

Students, in other words, need to be warned that they can't find their own way; that they can't rely on Blake authorities and that, none of the prophetic works is successful, anyway. It goes without saying that the final sentence is offered here as an explanation. Presumably, if the prophetic books were "successful" works of art, guidebooks would be plentiful and readers (even undergraduates) could be trusted to find their own bearings. That the prophecies are unlike anything else in the canon (excepting, perhaps *Revelation* and *Daniel*) is certainly true. But all of Blake's works, even the "successful" ones (which Leavis omits from his judgment with the qualifier "elaborated"), like *Songs of Innocence and of Experience* or *The Marriage of Heaven and Hell*, are unlike anything else in the canon. The unstated but inescapable assumption here is that Blake, though he began as a promising artist and even achieved some minor successes, soon fell victim to his eccentric religious views and his lack of formal education and artistic training. These factors, combined with the possibility of a certain mental instability, increasingly isolated him from his readers and resulted in his making unacceptable demands (both logical and aesthetic) on them. The consequence was the lack of success Leavis asserts.

This is not the place to relate the long and sad story of Blake's supposed madness or instability, but it is clear that that charge, whether openly stated or silently assumed, along with Leavis's seemingly more neutral aesthetic assessment supplies us with "good reasons" not to read and study Blake. But these reasons are, if examined, spurious. For all its seeming self-evidence, Leavis' assertion of aesthetic failure is both unsupported and unconvincing. Still, the difficulty faced, both by teacher and student of Blake, is real – even if its source lies no more in Blake's incapacity than in his originality. It lies, instead, in our unwillingness to read his works as he demands that they be read and to the end that he specifies. We are told, again and again, to read and experience his work with all our faculties, not simply with the reasoning one, and to do so to the purpose of our own, and our fellows' restoration: "Mark well my words! they are of your eternal salvation," is repeated, for example, no less than seven times in the opening plates of *Milton*.[30]

Blake explicitly instructs us not simply to "read" or "note" his words, but to actively *mark* them, that is, to attend to them with our whole being; with our emotional, physical, and intuitive faculties as well as the reasoning one. The editors of a standard text of Blake remind us of the importance of this level of concentration when they remark that, "…it is difficult to convert Blake's etched work into an accurate and readable printed text. One reason is that each copy Blake made is different from all the others…. Furthermore, Blake's spelling, capitalization, and especially punctuation are loose and eccentric, even for a time when such matters were not perfectly standardized." It is, in fact, not simply difficult "to convert" Blake into a "readable printed text," it is impossible because "…there are no typographical equivalents for such Blakean marks as oblong periods and elongated colons (or are they short exclamation points? lopped-off question marks?) and what of other exotic punctuation, such as the upper part of a question mark over a comma base? Or what is sometimes called his 'breathing stop,' – a dot raised above the line of the text and interrupting a grammatical unit? Or his birds, butterflies, squiggles, and plant tendrils?"[31] Each of us, then, must "mark" the words individually; must find the punctuation, sound and tempo that work for our time and place; and we must also integrate the "birds, butterflies, squiggles and plant tendrils," for all of these are of our "eternal salvation." Mark my words, he says, because they (when marked) are of *your* eternal salvation. It is hard to fault the poet here – at least it is so long as we refuse to heed his injunction.

These same editors note that no two "copies" of any of the "texts" are alike. They do not discuss what this might mean. They do say that others have labored to present what they take to be "final or preferred" texts from these variations. Again, the operative assumption here is that Blake intended or desired a text that was "perfectly standardized," in spite of the overwhelming and life long evidence, in his words and in his practice, that his goal was the realization of individual difference. Why should he wish for them to be perfect in their likeness when they were created, at different times, by – and for – different persons?

As to his wrestling, in his art, "against the rulers of the darkness of this world, against spiritual wickedness in high places," it follows that those rulers and that wickedness are well served in a world that dismisses him as an autodidact who, if not exactly paranoid was at least a little misguided and naive. But was Blake, in fact, this naive? Not in the least. In the Preface to *Milton,* he explicitly decries the ignorant "Hirelings in the Camp, the Court, & the University: who would if they could, for ever depress Mental & prolong Corporeal War."[32] By "Hirelings," he means those who labor for money and whose loyalty is neither to quality, truth nor art, but to cash. These hypocrites, especially those in high places, work against the construction of Jerusalem and seek to prolong as much as possible physical, that is Corporeal, war by their enforcement of the canons of taste and morality. Spiritual war, that is the vigorous debate arising from the discovery and publication of individual difference, is feared by them and, as much as possible, depressed. The art approved by such an "establishment," is ordered, rational, stable and resists the strange, the individual and the visionary. Blake vigorously rejected such art and the artists who promoted it. "The Man," as he wrote on the margins of his copy of Joshua Reynolds' *Works,* "who does not know The Beginning, never can know the End of Art."[33] The artist and the man who ignores three fourths of his reality cannot be expected to produce an art which does otherwise than teach by entertaining or vice versa.

Both the active agents of spiritual wickedness and their passive victims in the general population were seen by Blake as promoting a kind of unbelief and doubt which cripples the individual soul and degrades the culture.

> Many suppose that before the Creation All was Solitude & Chaos. This is the most pernicious Idea that can enter the Mind, as it takes away all sublimity from the Bible & Limits All Existence to Creation & to Chaos, To the Time & Space fixed by the Corporeal Vegetative Eye, & leaves the Man who entertains such an Idea the habitation of Unbelieving Demons. Eternity Exists, and All things in Eternity, Independent of Creation which was an act of Mercy.[34]

By limiting our existence to material cause and effect in time and space and to the random effect of colliding matter, we do, indeed, make ourselves, "the habitation of Unbelieving demons." Fortunately, according to Blake, this self-perpetuating and self-fulfilling cycle is countered by the body of Christ:

> …What seems to Be: Is: To those to whom
> It seems to Be, & is productive of the most dreadful
> Consequences to those to whom it seems to Be: even of
> Torments, Despair, Eternal Death; but the Divine Mercy
> Steps beyond and Redeems Man in the Body of Jesus Amen
> And Length Bredth Highth again Obey the Divine Vision
> Hallelujah[35]

What is meant here by Length Breadth and Height obeying Divine Vision is their return to the beauty of individual specification as opposed to the tyranny of the norm or average so idealized by rational systems. The beauty of the individual line and the value of its particular variation is specified in some remarks Blake made late in his life:

> I know too well that a great majority of Englishmen are fond
> of The Indefinite which they Measure by Newton's Doctrine
> of the Fluxions of an Atom, A Thing that does not Exist...
> For a Line or Lineament is not formed by Chance: a Line is
> a Line in its Minutest Subdivisions: Strait or Crooked It is
> Itself & Not Intermeasurable with or by any Thing Else.
> Such is Job, but since the French Revolution Englishmen
> are all Intermeasurable One by Another, Certainly a happy
> state of Agreement to which I for One do not Agree. God
> keep me from the Divinity of Yes & No too, the Yea Nay
> Creeping Jesus, from supposing Up & Down to be the same
> Thing as all Experimentalists must suppose.[36]

What Blake sees in the world and seeks to capture in his art is that idiosyncratic detail in individual "lineaments" which marks each created thing. The many who, like him, labor in the actual moment, plowing in tears, can hear the voices in the clouds of heaven,

> Crying: Compel the Reasoner to Demonstrate with unhewn
>   Demonstrations.
> Let the Indefinite be explored, and let every Man be Judged
> By his own Works. Let all Indefinites be thrown into
>   Demonstrations
> To be pounded to dust & melted in the furnaces of Affliction.
> He who would do good to another must do it in Minute
>   Particulars:
> General Good is the plea of the scoundrel, hypocrite &
>   flatterer,
> For Art & Science cannot exist but in minutely organized
>   Particulars
> And not in generalizing Demonstrations of the Rational
>   Power.[37]

Blake's allusion here to Exodus 20:25 ["And if thou wilt make me an altar of stone, thou shalt not build it of hewn stone: for if thou lift up thy tool upon it, thou hast polluted it."] suggests that it refers to the gifts of the imagination. For most of his contemporaries, the imagination consisted in the mind's capacity to combine various things which, in nature, are never found together and would, in the context of Blake's reading here, be the equivalent of a 'hewn' or polluted stone. The pollution, in this case, being the egoistic reasoner's imposition of his own order on the world, as in the Deists' argument that, since the Gods are no more than creatures of the imagination, it is absurd to prefer any of them and, indeed, the best picture of God would be the most abstract. Against such relativism and abstraction, Blake sets the power of the particular in the unhewn stone of the divine Imagination or vision. When Blake says that, "The antiquities of every Nation under Heaven, is no less sacred than that of the Jews,"[38] he doesn't mean that they're all more or less imperfect variants of a perfectly abstract original. He means that each is an unhewn stone, each is equally, and individually sacred, just as each person is a sacred member of Christ. The heavenly voices here might be paraphrased as follows: Demand that Reasoners bring to the struggle not abstract theories, statistics and models, but rather "unhewn," that is, particular examples, persons with names, addresses and histories.[39] Let all hypotheses be ground into dust and let judgment be passed on each person according to his tangible, present and actual works, for the only goodness is a tangible, real gift, given by a tangible, real person.

That the Imagination is "Unhewn," of course, doesn't mean that we don't work on our art with all our powers. Indeed, each vowel and consonant of the poem, each line, each mass of the sculpture, each aspect of the design of the painting can only exist in 'minutely organized Particulars.' What is unhewn, then, is not the poem, sculpture or painting, but the Divine Vision which is its source and which it tries to realize. The judgment that is passed on each of us is on our poem, sculpture, painting or performance. For each of us is here to realize only a part – that part given each individually by the "Poetic Genius" or the "Eternal Great Humanity Divine."[40]

Thus Blake is totally opposed to that universalism praised by the neoclassicists like Samuel Johnson and Joshua Reynolds. Their view of art understood individual variation to be the result of chance and so they removed from their art precisely that element which Blake valued most highly. Out of similarly reductive operations came also the

tyranny of social/religious "norms" – what Blake refers to so marvel-
ously here as "the Yea Nay creeping Jesus." A rational, relativist model
of grace and goodness might, indeed, satisfy reason's requirements –
but nothing could be further than that norm from the unique, concrete
salvation we truly desire.

And Blake not only rejects reason's centrality to our individual happiness and success; he also specifically denies the notion that either
God or the cosmos is bound or constrained by it. The notion that either God, or man, or the world in which we find ourselves is somehow
"reasonable," or governed by reason, is manifestly absurd to Blake:

> What it will be Questiond When the Sun rises do you not
> see a round Disk of fire somewhat like a Guinea   O no no
> I see an Innumerable company of the Heavenly host crying
> Holy Holy Holy is the Lord God Almighty   I question not
> my Corporeal or Vegetative Eye any more than I would
> Question a Window concerning a Sight   I look thro it & not
> with it.[41]

Note that Blake doesn't *deny* reason; he is here quite clearly reasoning with his reader. First there is the experiment (regard the rising
sun), then the results: (1) a physical image, the bright round disk of fire
about Guinea size in the sky, and, (2) the visionary company, an immediate and intuitive sense that what is apprehended here is a source
not merely of light and heat, but of life itself. This second vision is expansive and complex, not reductive and simple, and it bursts the limitations of the material – what Blake calls 'vegetative' – world. Blake
sees a company calling "Holy Holy"; in other words, he hears with his
eyes. He explains this naturally and easily by analogy: just as what we
see through a window is infinitely more real and present than the lines
and colors caught on the pane, so the innumerable host singing us all
into being shines through the surface brightness of our nearby star.

Blake does not dismiss reason; nor does he deny the material world.
Of course what one sees is a flaming disk in the sky. But he vehemently
denies the claim of *exclusive* reality by the reasoning faculty for the
material – what he calls, the "vegetative" – world. In other words, he
does not deny either reason or the text of reality; of course there is a

text. But the words are not the meaning; the text is NOT the poem. Actual experience, if you consult it, says Blake will confirm that the song is more than the notes; the painting more than the line and color – and your own life is much more than material cause and effect. You were not reasoned into being; ask your parents. You were thought, dreamed, imagined, sung and danced together into being.

Fortunately, the ubiquity of reason's reduction of value to number, and of charity to statistics, doesn't finally convince. Mercifully, we cling to the people we love regardless of their market value. We may not be logical in this; we may not be prudent or politic; but when we find it, we cannot relinquish the reality of love. And it is precisely to this reality that Blake appeals:

> What is it men in women do require
> The lineaments of Gratified Desire

> What is it women do in men require
> The lineaments of Gratified Desire[42]

The answer to the question – "What is Love?" – is not "more"; it is not even "the most." The answer is "The lineaments of Gratified Desire."

The scholars seem in agreement that *ALL RELIGIONS are ONE* is the opening and fundamental work in Blake's "illuminated" canon.[43] This tiny "book," exists, fittingly, in a single copy. The first plate reveals a muscular, partially clothed young man, seated, with the right leg crossed over the left, facing the viewer and pointing, with both arms, at (what appears to be) the blank face of a rock on the further side of a flowing stream (to his left). Beneath the image are the words of Isaiah, as quoted by John the Baptist: "The Voice of one crying in the Wilderness."[44] Blake's spiritual stance, his subject matter and method, could hardly be more clearly, or economically, stated. Still, the two little (2 x 2 & 1/2 inch) sets of copperplate etchings that follow – *ALL RELIGIONS are ONE* and *THERE is NO NATURAL RELIGION* – are often overlooked. More importantly, it is not often noticed how carefully reasoned (as opposed to "mystical" or "prophetic") the following paragraphs (or axioms) are:

The Argument

As the true meth-
-od of knowledge
is experiment
the true faculty
of knowing must
be the faculty which
experiences, This
faculty I treat of.

Principle 1st
That the Poetic Genius is
the true Man.   and that
the body or outward form
of Man is derived from the
Poetic Genius.[45]

Note that the 'faculty' or capacity to experience is *not* the reasoning faculty. For we experience reality all the time, not only when we reason about it. It is certainly true to my experience that I often employ my reasoning capacity as a tool to get (or try to get) what I want. And it is equally true that I frequently reason myself into believing I want something, only to learn when I get it that I really didn't want it at all. In a "reasonable" world, it seems particularly cruel or ironic that I am able to "reason" myself into a state of dissatisfaction. But, of course, ours isn't a world of reason. Existence is not a thing (static); it is a song (process). The principal of reality for Blake, then, is not logical (reductive), but poetic (generative). We are wanting creatures and what we want is not "more," try as we may to convince ourselves that it is. What we want is "Gratified Desire." What we want is nothing less than the Truth.

In what follows, Blake examines this thirst – and its resolution:

Mans perceptions are not bounded by organs of perception.
he percieves more than sense (tho' ever so acute) can discover.

…More! More! is the cry of a mistaken soul, less than All cannot satisfy Man.

If any could desire what he is incapable of possessing, despair must be his eternal lot.

The desire of Man being Infinite the possession is Infinite & himself Infinite.

Conclusion.   If it were not for the Poetic or Prophetic character. the Philosophic & Experimental would soon be at the ratio of all things & stand still, unable to do other than repeat the same dull round over again[46]

The importance here of the Imagination, the Poetic or Prophetic character, does not, however, suggest or require that imaginative vision is prior to, or "more real than," what is perceived. Nor does it deny the very important role of reason. All that is denied is the worship of reason. For Blake understands perception to be not a passive matter of the reception of the material world, but the active process of playing host to all we perceive, with our senses, our imagination, our reason and our intuition. His stress is always on our active and joyful participation in the miracle of quotidian experience. His works, by grounding themselves in actual experience, don't so much direct readers to the historical (and abstract) 'issues' of his times[47] as they exhort us all to attend to the necessity of apprehending the truth in our own lives, of the importance, that is, not only of going to the wedding feast, but of remembering to bring with us "a wedding garment."[48] The point is not that miraculous events occur from time to time and place to place but that this life itself, every breath, is miraculous, for:

The Eye sees more than the Heart knows.[49]

Read that again. Didn't you think, "Wait a minute; I thought the point of all this visionary perception was that the heart saw more than the eye." What is Blake saying here? And Blake, indeed, means for you to pause here. And reason. For the eye that sees through the surface to the infinite and the eternal, does, indeed, see more than even the heart knows. For it is then what it is intended to be: a window connecting the heart to its source which is the innumerable host of Heaven. That, I think, is why in those moments it fills with tears. For Blake does *not* suggest that "the answer is within," as do so many of our so-called 'seers' and mystics.

If we carried the truth within us, we could find it alone; there would be no necessity for others – and no difference between us and that oddly jealous and self-sufficient God Blake identifies as Milton's and the Church's "Governor or Reason...calld Messiah."[50] Instead, says Blake, we must labor to construct the truth, together. Reason, though a necessary discipline for the attainment of clarity, is not clarity's self. And though certainty is an element in the recognition of truth, truth, itself, is not certain. Those determined to have certainty cling to doubt as their means to its attainment. They come, that is, to the wedding feast – but without a wedding garment.[51] The artist and the prophet, on the other hand, is continually trying, always believing in that illumination – that connection to eternity – which is deeper even than the heart knows. He has his wedding garment with him at every moment! Of course, his most common experience is defeat and failure. And nothing sustains him in this defeat but his belief in that connection. Nothing matters but that eternal moment. And when we, to whom the artist's and prophet's work are directed, are unable to attain the connection with eternity our disappointment is no greater than his. Like him, we must try. And try again.

If we are confused by Blake's art and puzzled by his stubborn refusal to make it easily accessible (and we are), then it seems only fair to grant that he may have known what he was doing, that he was aware of our difficulty and puzzlement. We can continue to read him as rationalists – and dismiss him as a failure. Or we can reconsider our way of reading. In Blake's time the quarrel about how to read the Bible was particularly loud and noisy. It was the rise of what Bible scholars call "historical criticism," application to the study of the Bible of the (then emerging) principals of linguistics and the "science" of history. Blake's position in the quarrel is clear and unambiguous. The Bible is art – and like any art, it is not addressed to the kind of reasoning idiot (or worse) he shows the good Bishop Watson to be:

> Nothing can be more contemptible than to suppose Public
> RECORDS to be True   Read, them & Judge. if you are
> not a Fool. Of what consequence is it whether Moses wrote
> the Pentateuch or no.... if it is True Moses & none but he
> could write it unless we allow it to be Poetry & that poetry in-
> spired If historical facts can be written by inspiration Miltons
> Paradise Lost is as true as Genesis. or Exodus.[52]

"Unless we allow it to be Poetry & that poetry inspired" – here is
the crux, for when we understand poetry we understand that "historical facts can be written by inspiration." For poetry, art, and the
Bible – all grand works of the imagination are addressed not alone to
the reasoning faculty but to all the faculties. And Blake's dismissal of
(purely) rational criticism is succinct: "His opinions, who does not see
spiritual agency, is not worth any man's reading."[53] How then are we to
proceed with Blake? It's one thing to say that your work is addressed to
all the faculties, but shouldn't you provide a little help to the beginner?
The bluntness and complexity of Blake's work, from the *Songs* through
Jerusalem have provoked numerable complaints about the inaccessibility of his myth and the lack of a reliable guide to it. These complaints
began in his lifetime, and though he refused to address them in the
works themselves, he did respond in a letter to one of his complain-
ers, which – God be thanked! – the addressee, a Reverend Dr. Trusler,
preserved:

> You say that I want somebody to Elucidate my Ideas. But you
> ought to know that What is Grand is necessarily obscure to
> Weak men. That which can be made Explicit to the Idiot is
> not worth my care. The wisest of the Ancients considerd what
> is not too Explicit as the fittest for Instruction because it
> rouzes the faculties to act.[54]

What is not too explicit is fittest for instruction. If it can be easily "elucidated," it will fail to "rouse the faculties to act." Blake's art,
that is, is addressed to those seeking instruction, not answers. And

the instruction is individual and intuitive, not general and deductive because the faculties to be roused are spiritual ones. Blake believes that, "Knowledge is not by deduction but Immediate by Perception or Sense at once Christ addresses himself to the Man not to his Reason Plato did not bring Life & Immortality to Light Jesus only did this."[55] This opposition of Plato to Jesus, analysis to apprehension, is fundamental to any reading of Blake. We are accustomed to analyzing arguments and texts rationally; it's what you are doing right now. It's what you have been trained in from the beginning. But Blake makes greater (and other) demands.

If we only come to the truth by the spirit; if it is the uniquely spiritual in art to which we respond, and not the abstract and rational, then it follows that all true art is provocative, catalytic. And the changes or processes it intends will take place in the individual member of the audience, not in the homogeneous mass. But who are these individuals? Are they limited to believers? Christians? The learned? You won't be surprised to learn that Blake was no Cabbalist:

> Jesus supposes every Thing to be Evident to the Child & to the Poor & Unlearned Such is the Gospel

> The Whole Bible is filled with Imaginations & Visions from End to End & not with Moral Virtues that is the baseness of Plato & the Greeks & all Warriors The Moral Virtues are continual Accusers of Sin & promote Eternal Wars & Domineering over others[56]

Now if everything is evident to the child, the poor and unlearned, then Blake's art, like the Gospel, must be also available to all. But availability does not presuppose transparency. Remember, "That which can be made Explicit to the Idiot is not worth my care."[57] True art becomes evident through the rousing of all the faculties, not via the reasoning power alone. At this point you may, like my students, be impatient and asking, "What faculties other than reason can he be talking about? If I had any such faculties wouldn't I have discovered them by now?"

No. Nor will you discover them here. The ideas I hope to provoke can no more be fully assimilated in isolation than they could have been so generated.[58] This book is assembled from what I have learned through and with my students. To make use of it, you will need to read it with and through others. For instance, Blake identifies four agencies or faculties, internal to each of us, which he calls the Four Zoas after the "four living creatures" of Ezekiel.[59] Though they are present in each of us, they are also uniquely and individually unbalanced – and a considerable effort is required to bring them into balance. Nor, since they are dynamic, will they stay balanced for long. The Zoas, with the help of our human companions, will assist us in that recovery and recreation of one another and reality which Blake calls the building of Jerusalem. Of course no one may be required to participate, for participation requires, in this case, belief – and belief cannot be compelled. Nor can the task be completed without the assistance of every one of us. The slightest inattention or lapse in any one of us is registered, is felt, by all. And, to make "sense" of Blake, we need every bow, every arrow, every spear and every chariot. In the following chapters, I supply some techniques which have helped myself and others to begin the task. But first, I need to introduce the Zoas, with the names[60] Blake assigns them:

Reason (Urizen) is the easiest to remember. I ask my students to think about the fact that they so quickly recognize this Zoa and his name. He is your thinking faculty, that which asks: Is it coherent? organized? logical and orderly? Or is it chaotic? inconsistent and confused? Urizen's is the realm of syntax and formula, of language and logic, of grammar and mathematics. There Science lives; in the proving and disproving; in the prediction and control of things. (But to what end?)

Feeling or Emotion (Luvah) is next. We have been trained to suppress our emotion on the grounds that it interferes with judgment. Some have believed that they are capable of this suppression. When we encounter these people we, wisely, give them a wide berth. When you are performing a task, you should notice and respect your feelings: Does it make you anxious? Or does it bore you? Are you jealous? Or generous? Do you feel welcomed? Or threatened? Are tears threatening to flow? Or giggles? Our feelings, of course, are deeper and far more complex than our language for them and their force is mightily particular and more immediately present than any theorem. Are they really disruptive? Of what? And why?

Sensation is, oddly, the least recognized of the four, though he is the most constantly present. Blake calls him Tharmas. I think, later, you'll see why. For now you need only answer these and similar questions to get a handle on him: Is it smooth or rough? Dark or bright? Loud or soft? Dissonant or harmonious? Sweet or sour? Does your skin tingle? Or is it clammy? Consult your elbows and your toes; run your tongue across your fingertips. What do you HEAR, SEE, SMELL, TASTE and TOUCH? Supply details. Be as specific as a pin-prick and never say it doesn't matter; the matter is exactly what it is!

Finally comes Intuition or Imagination, which Blake calls Urthona. Again, I believe in time you'll see why.[61] When you say "Yes!" or "Yuck!" it is this faculty which supplies your awareness of the wholeness/rightness or the lack/wrongness of whatever is presented by your experience. Artists are famously tongue-tied when asked to explain this agent – as well they might be. In the first place it is not exclusively theirs; everyone has it. And in the second place, it is the wellspring of that peculiar identity or signature by which we recognize one another.

These Four, together, are not who you want to be, or who you think you are or should be; they are who you (forever) are. At the beginning of *Milton*, Blake calls them to the task. We need to call them as well, for the task, as one of Blake's more famous lyric specifies, is ours: we (with and through one another) are the builders here. Now:

> Bring me my Bow of burning gold: (Urizen)
> Bring me my Arrows of desire: (Luvah)
> Bring me my Spear: O clouds unfold! (Tharmas)
> Bring me my Chariot of fire! (Urthona)

> I will not cease from Mental Fight,
> Nor shall my Sword sleep in my hand:
> Till we have built Jerusalem,
> In Englands green & pleasant Land.[62]

Two: In the Palm of Your Hand

He who wishes to see a Vision, a perfect Whole
Must see it in Minute Particulars, Organized…

WILLIAM BLAKE, *Jerusalem* 91: 21-2

There's something you need to know about my blind student, Jackie: hers is not the face of someone who can't see. It's true that her eyes, open and sparkling, didn't focus and wandered only vaguely in the direction of my voice. But – and this is the part you have to grasp – they were smiling. At me. Her whole face was lit with enthusiasm. So, when I had finished explaining to her that we were going to pay a great deal of attention to the visual aspect of Blake's work, using watercolors to finish some designs and also carving, printing, and coloring a linoleum block, I couldn't tell when she nodded, whether she was agreeing with me or signaling to someone behind me that she'd be with him in a minute. I even looked over my shoulder to check.

Maybe I could sing.

Sing? I said, and a cloud passed across her face. She read my ignorance in that single syllable and immediately came to my rescue.

Or if I could tape record the lectures and type out my notes later; I have a Braille typewriter. Then, instead of water coloring and carving, maybe I could do something…in writing?

Well, I guess – Do you mean, reports? Or extra papers?

I thought meditations might be nice. She was smiling directly at me. And before I could think of how to respond, her student assistant was wheeling her toward the classroom. So I followed – and called the roll for the first meeting. Oh yes, I forgot: her illness had affected her nervous system as well as her sight, so she was chair bound as well as blind. A week later, at the second meeting, when the others were turning in their first assignment, Jackie asked if she could read us her first meditation. Her clear voice filled the room:

Meditation Number One

Why look for me in mountains far,
When you can find me where you are?
For my existence you can see
In every plant and every tree
In every tiny grain of sand
And every flower upon the land.

Eternity begins here and now;
So, within your heart, please vow
To understand this truth somehow
And look not with – but through – faith's eyes,
For this is how you realize
That an hour and eternity are one
As God the Father and the Son.[1]

People asked for copies. She was blind and chair bound, yes. But she was busy laying the foundations of Jerusalem for us. Soon the class was shaping and collecting similarly useful bits. We followed the syllabus for the rest of the semester but, more importantly, we also followed Jackie.

One writer has noted a "naked intensity one often senses rather than grasps," in Blake's work.[2] And I think it's best to begin with Blake by discussing the part the Four Zoas play in that sensing and awareness. For they are not in us as poetic fictions, concepts or ideas; the Zoas are wound in the fibers of our being, as present as our heartbeats – and as taken for granted. Getting "in touch" with them, then, is best managed not by a lecture or description, but by an exercise, an inner exploration which calls them into action. And so, before I assign any reading involving the names of the Zoas or their struggles, I try to get my students to come, through their own experience, to an awareness of them. Because once you know who they are and where they live, it's easy to learn their names.

Further, since I can't count on Jackie to model true seeing every time I offer Blake, I decided that in subsequent courses I would give the students (at the first meeting), a Blake design to "illuminate."[3] I use a simple one, with no accompanying text. **[See Figure #1]** It is centered on the sheet so that the decision about which is the top must be each person's own. My instructions are that they should begin by considering whether or not the assignment requires the use of watercolors. It may, for instance, seem to them better to employ pastels, or crayons, or acrylics, or oils, or some combination of these and/or other things. I explain that I prefer watercolors because they're so hard to predict and manage – but not everyone likes that feeling. So long as that result is an illumination of the design, nothing is either required or forbidden. When asked, I tell them to check their dictionary for "illuminate." The rest of the assignment, however, has detailed and very specific requirements. Each student must keep a written record of the process of illumination, and turn it in along with their finished product. In this recording each begins to realize what "paying attention" really means, and (although not at first!) how "an hour and eternity are one."

This record must include (but is not limited to) detailed responses to whatever in the following seems pertinent: 1. What do I think I'm doing? What plans or goals do I have? What methods for achieving them? And what specific assumptions, or systems of assumptions, am I relying on to direct my choices; how do I know, in other words, whether I've made a mistake or not? 2. How do I feel about what I'm doing and thinking? When I list these feelings or emotions, what other ones am I aware of that I don't want to confess? Am I aware of any shifts in feeling as the process goes forward: frustration, satisfaction, boredom, excitement, fear, joy, sorrow? What caused them? Are there feelings I can't find words for? If so, what are they "like"? Are there colors or details in my illumination that express my feeling(s) better than words? 3. What are the physical circumstances under which this process is going forward? Am I hungry? full? tired? alert? Is the room cold? hot? Is the light bright or dim? Natural or artificial? What sounds can I hear? What smells or tastes do I notice? What part(s) of my body am I conscious of? 4. Finally, what "hunches" or "inspirations" are directing or contributing to this process? What choices or decisions did I make that "just felt" right? Did I make any mistakes that lead me to something surprising?

I look forward to the first set of Illuminations in the course, because grading them is so much fun – and so easy. They almost always forget to record what they intuited and what they were feeling emotionally and physically during the process. So I cheerfully award Ds and Fs, having, for once, found a good use for their strong attachment to grades; the marks get their attention and reveal to them how casually, unthinkingly, they ignore the precise details of their experience and replace them with vague abstractions. Many, for instance, short-change Urizen, by supplying rote or cliché reasons like: I made the fire yellow and orange because fire is yellow and orange. In addition to awarding the low grades, I point out, as gently as possible, that: (a), fire isn't always only yellow, orange or red; and (b), that wavy lines do not automatically equal "fire." Some list emotions, but most insist they didn't have time for them (I was really too busy to feel very much.) Too busy doing what? I ask, reminding them that not noting emotions is not the same thing as not having them. The same holds true for their physical sensations and intuitions.

On the subsequent illumination assignments they become increasingly proficient at noting, and acknowledging, the presence and power of the Zoas in their creative work – and in their lives. Two things are accomplished by asking them to record these details as well as illuminate the design: first, because the reasoning faculty is very good at noting, cataloging, listing details, and *completing* things, it is delighted to take on the difficult task of monitoring and attending; second, as they attend to the myriad contributions of their sensations, emotions and intuitions in the construction of reality, they become aware of the importance of paying attention, both to one another and themselves. That's the end of easy grading!

Figure 1

While I was wrestling with the problem of grading student work in the Blake course, I realized I had come back, after all these years, to O.B. Hardison's original question, the one that started all my adventures with Blake: Why do these poems so blatantly ignore the structural and other requirements of their genre? Why does he deliberately refuse in them to clarify the reader's role in the preservation of the structure and values of his society? Why, in simpler terms, doesn't he follow the examples of Homer, Virgil and Milton? The answer must be, at least in part, that it is precisely those structures and values he wishes the reader to examine rather than take for granted. His poems are provocations, whose purpose (like Lao Tsu's verses) is to teach the reader that he must teach himself – and begin this by *listening to himself.* They are, in other words, deliberate rejections of the notion that truth or meaning are social constructions and the individual's task is agreement with them. What Blake demands of readers is *an act of judgment*, something he has labeled "Mental" or "Spiritual" war.[4] This is a dynamic process in which each person finds not only a necessary element of his or her own salvation, but that of every other person as well. And this Judgment, this salvation for Blake is not eschatological, or removed from this life; it is now and here, at this (very) moment and in this (very) place.[5] Thus, when he addresses the reader and calls her to assist in the construction of "Jerusalem / In England's green & pleasant land,"[6] he doesn't have an imperial or nationalistic enterprise in mind. Instead he envisions a minutely detailed realization of the Holy City in "the green and pleasant" beauty of this, our actual, world. If ever there were a task to be graded finally and only by its participants, it is this one!

And since we are not here to passively enter and enjoy some *ideal* Jerusalem as a reward for our correct responses, but to actively construct and celebrate *our own* Jerusalem, the only one there is or can be, we will not "want either Greek or Roman Models if we are but just & true to our own Imaginations, those Worlds of Eternity in which we shall live for ever in Jesus our Lord."[7] The individual nature of the judgment is explicit here: we will need no models – but only if we are "just & true to our own Imaginations." Our task, in short, is to "Read ... & judge" – that is build in our time and in our lives that which has waited for precisely our hands, our feelings and our vision.[8]

A critic might be compelled to interrupt here that such a program invites chaos by allowing (indeed, by seeming to require) total freedom, the probable consequence being that readers (or students), allowed to simply follow their own preference, will arrive at trivializations of the text by lazily taking the path of least resistance. And, how, such a critic might well demand of me, can you presume to grade such efforts? Leaving aside the manifold problems inherent in the concept of grading, let me suggest that it is, indeed, obvious that some students will avoid real work and seek to conceal that avoidance with cliché or assertions of sincerity. But avoidance and its cloak of cliché and insincerity is hardly something limited to a Blake course. Some students make a career of taking the path of least resistance, flattering the teacher with copies, imitations and/or parodies of his lectures and readings.[9] But

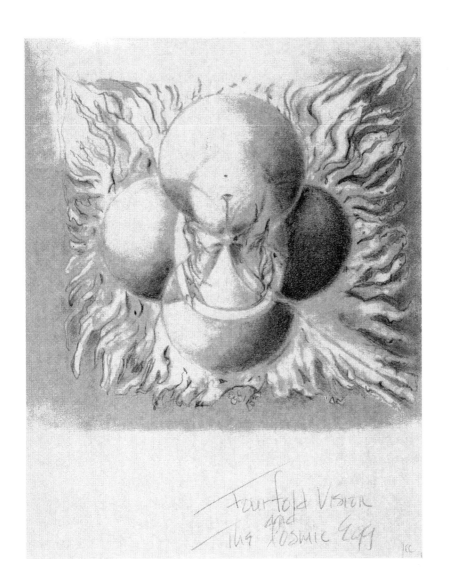

Fourfold Vision
and
The Cosmic Egg

neither teacher nor student is really satisfied for, though the teacher is
flattered and the student receives a "passing grade," neither gets the
satisfaction of really speaking – or really being heard. In Blake's terms,
the city they are building is Babylon, not Jerusalem.

But being made to defend a cliché with respect to the work of Blake
is an exquisitely uncomfortable position in which to place oneself. For
he insists not only that you "read & judge" him, but that you do so
in truth and justice to your own imagination.[10] No teacher can say
that a student is not true to his own imagination, that's a given – but
it is also a given that the student cannot say he is true to his imagination when he isn't – *and not know it.* Saying that you are speaking your
mind when you know that you aren't is a strain; but saying aloud to
the teacher and your fellow students that you are speaking your mind,
heart and soul when you know you are lying is excruciating. Anything
accomplished by this means – especially when others are impressed by
it – is immediately devalued by your awareness of its meanness. On
the other hand, actually speaking your heart, mind, body and soul is as
rewarding and liberating an experience as you are like to have in this
life. Blake makes this point in his examination of the Prophet Isaiah in
The Marriage of Heaven and Hell:

> Then I asked: "does a firm perswasion that a thing is so,
> make it so?"
> He replied: "All poets believe that it does, & in ages of
> imagination this firm perswasion removed mountains; but
> many are not capable of a firm perswasion of any thing."[11]

A firm persuasion, let it be noted, is a belief arrived at only by an
act of individual judgment; no one can supply it for you. And though
it is true that many are not capable of a firm persuasion, it is less from
incapacity than a lack of experience. But how are we to find such an
experience? It is one thing to propose it, even to insist on it – it is quite
another to make it possible.

Blake scholars will have recognized that the design for the first
Illumination assignment is derived from his diagram of the Four Zoas
on plate 32 of *Milton.*[12] The line curving from the lower right corner
into the center of the design is there labeled "Miltons Track." The

Zoas, also labeled, are constellated in their "unfallen" relationship[13] with Urthona at the top or North; Tharmas on the left or West; Luvah, right and East; and Urizen to the South, or bottom. In addition, the names "Adam" and "Satan" are placed in the upper and lower portions of the egg. By asking the students to illuminate this bare diagram before they have learned anything about Blake's myth or have even thought much about the four fold nature of their perceptions, I am forcing them to rely on their spontaneous reactions by making it both difficult and pointless to rely on anything else. Why should a person lie about, or fake, this task when she doesn't really know what she's doing?

Later, when we begin dealing directly with the Zoas, both in ourselves and in Blake, the members of the class have some valuable data stored in these early illuminations: for this was what they were able to do before they began to limit themselves with labels and expectations. What they behold in these Illuminations is, inescapably, themselves. And that's where Blake requires each of us to start: where we are. Not where we're supposed to be, or where we'd like to be, but where we are. For, unless we make our judgments from this place, the only one true to our whole being, our time with Blake is wasted.

Suppose, for example, that the following paragraph accompanied a student's illumination of the Zoa diagram:

> To begin with, I'm mildly embarrassed at the thought some-
> one may discover me wasting my time on such quasi-mystical
> nonsense. I'm aware that the light is good in here, steady and
> bright – and artificial (standard fluorescent dorm lighting).
> The room is about 70 degrees, there's no breeze; I can hear
> the furnace click on and off intermittently; and there's some
> rock music drifting down the hall and under my door. I'm con-
> vinced that this information is wholly random and unrelated
> to either (a) myself or (b) this task. Finally, I'm conscious that
> there's absolutely no reason I should waste much time or effort
> on it: it makes no difference whether I paint the whole thing
> green – or just spatter some green on it and turn it in. On the
> other hand, since it's supposed to "illuminate" something, I
> have a hunch that wouldn't be a good idea. And I'm aware,
> too, that my indifference to this entire project is likely to be

(mis?) interpreted as hostility.

Since Blake argues that our Zoas are mostly in disarray and imbalance, and that the acquisition of a four-fold vision and the successful
building of Jerusalem requires us not only to bring them into balance,
but also to assist others in the same task, such a clear response is not
only to be expected – it is to be welcomed! For this person has spelled
out very clearly where she is. And unless we begin where we are, our
efforts to balance are doomed. Without a horizon in sight, we could be
in the kind of deadly spin, which killed so many pilots in the early days
of aviation. But an awareness like this person's, and the design that
comes with it, establishes clearly where she is. Coming back to our illuminations and records of our process is like finding old diary entries: in
them, we can see both our search – and what was blocking it. Viewing
another's illumination is just as revealing and just as helpful.

Indeed, the most important response students have to their illumination exercises is not their irritation at my grades, which disap-
pears rapidly with their understanding of what's required of them.
No, when they bring their illuminations to class, I lay them all on my
desktop. And what happens is very interesting: individuals are unfailingly drawn to the work of persons they had before not even noticed.
Discussions begin eagerly and move rapidly from the illuminations to
other aspects of their lives; commonalties are discovered with pleasure
– and it takes considerable effort to quiet things down and get on with
our work![14]

Part of what is happening in these encounters is that the dissatisfaction each person has with his own work is quickly overwhelmed by
the deep pleasures he takes in what others have done, facing the same
problem and working with the same design. For, when we look at our
own work we are acutely conscious of the disparity between what we
had hoped for and what we were able to achieve, but when we look
at others', we find solutions that hadn't occurred to us and beauties
they can't see because, like us, all they see are their failures. This is the
beginning of the creation of a community based on shared searching rather than inherited prejudices. And it includes an invaluable discovery: that knowing is not acquiring, but surrendering and that real
knowledge is found in the giving, not in the taking.

Blake knew both kinds of knowing, that which is acquired painfully and jealously guarded and that which is joyfully discovered in sharing, and he leaves no doubt as to which is to be preferred: "Plato has made Socrates say that Poets & Prophets do not Know or Understand what they write or Utter. This is a most pernicious Falsehood. If they do not, pray, is an inferior Kind to be calld Knowing?"[15] He has little use for academies or cabals, especially their presumption that they are the sole source of truth. He was protesting the arrogance of the Scribes and Pharisees when he said to Henry Crabb Robinson: "There is no use in education. I hold it wrong – It is the great Sin; it is eating of the tree of the knowledge of good & evil. That was the fault of Plato – he knew of nothing but of the Virtues & Vices and good & evil. There is nothing in all that – Everything is good in God's eyes."[16] His curt dismissal of ethics or morality – "There is nothing in that" – is based on his belief that good and evil, which he said Jesus believed, are evident to a child,[17] actually exist only in "minute particulars;"[18] and are therefore recognized immediately by the Zoas (Intuition, Emotion, Sensation and Reason) working in concert – not acquired from outside by instruction.

Concepts of abstract good and evil, of beauty and justice lead inevitably to their commodification and, ultimately desire itself is commodified. "More! More!," Blake wrote, "is the cry of a mistaken soul. Less than All cannot satisfy Man."[19] This, he continues, is because, "The desire of Man being Infinite, the possession is Infinite & himself Infinite."[20] Neglecting this infinitude leads us to construct gradations and hierarchies, things which do not really exist. On the other hand, when we work in community, beginning exactly where we are and granting to all the same privilege, we are enabled to escape the limiting bounds of codes and law:[21]

> I   Mans perceptions are not bounded by organs of perception. he percieves more than sense (tho' ever so acute) can discover.
> II   Reason or the ratio of all we have already known. is not the same that it shall be when we know more.
>
> IV   The bounded is loathed by its possessor. The same

dull round even of a universe would soon become a mill with complicated wheels.[22]

The Illumination exercises, which are carried out over several weeks, then, not only teach the value of shared struggle but also how crucial it is that we do the best we can with what we really have. Here. And now. Obsessing about what we *would* do, or *could* do with something we imagine to be absent, is doubting, or not believing that all we need *is* at hand. The unspoken complaint of the perfectionist is that the God he purports to worship has been deficient in supplying him with the materials he needs to complete that worship. He sees mistakes as proof of inadequacy rather than opportunities, unexpected gifts. He can't hear "the voice of the Bard,"[23] because he is listening to another, smoother one. It comes from the (inflated) Ego, what Blake calls "the limit of opakeness,"[24] emphasizing its self-generated refusal to acknowledge the divine continuity and unity of creation. As the Zoa diagram reveals, Satan lives inside each of us.[25] He is the "Selfhood," proclaiming isolation, declaring the impossibility of our participation in the building of Jerusalem, and demanding, instead, that we submit to and worship him – and him alone.[26] Casting out the Selfhood/Satan is, necessarily, an individual act or choice, and is the subject of Blake's *Milton.*[27] But first, we must locate and identify him – and for that we need help, "for a Man Can only Reject Error by the Advice of a Friend or by the Immediate Inspiration of God," as Blake writes in his description of his painting of the Last Judgment, "it is for this Reason...that I have put the Lords Supper on the Left hand of the Throne for it appears so at the Last Judgment for a Protection."[28] That Blake means by "the Advice of a Friend," something rather more active, communal, and difficult than simple instruction may be seen in the following verses:

> & Throughout all Eternity
> I forgive you you forgive me
> As our dear Redeemer said
> This the Wine & this the Bread[29]

For Blake, then, "The Lord's Supper," the Eucharist IS communion, and involves us all (you, me, and our Redeemer) in active forgiveness.

From the beginning of the course, students must keep a journal/notebook, so-called because it is neither the one nor the other. Each one's form and content are individually determined; in them we find what is discovered by looking through rather than with the eyes, and what is heard by ears that are open to listening. And there, too, we discover that, "Error is Created; Truth is Eternal; Error or Creation will be Burned Up, & then & not till then, Truth or Eternity will appear."[30] The journal/notebooks record our created Error(s) and, by showing us our mistakes, make possible our mutual discovery of the truth in our lives. When I am pressed for more details – as I always am when I announce that the journal/notebook accounts for twenty percent of the semester grade – I reply that it's impossible for *me* to say what will work for *you;* that you have to consult the Zoas, that you'll want something that feels good – physically and emotionally – and something that your reason is comfortable with, but also something that leaves room for inspiration. Other than that, experience suggests that the journal/notebook expands rather alarmingly to fill up all your available time and then begins stealing time that isn't available, so you'll probably want to get something bigger than you think you'll need.

Students must exchange journals each week for a couple of days – and each reader must respond physically and permanently, leaving a signed record (Marking well the words) in his partner's journal. Each is thus woven together with the others. And the more strands woven in and through it, the stronger it – and all the others! – will be. The overall structure, then, is not built by individuals laboring in isolation, but, like the Gothic cathedrals, by a community, full of division and argument, false starts, setbacks, errors and confusions. But, again like the Gothic churches Blake so loved, an organic harmony emerges greater than any Classical Ideal. And while each contributor becomes more, and more boldly, individual, the journal/notebooks become more and more obviously vital members of a whole. As each individual voice is clarified, the harmony of all the voices rings out:

And they conversed together in Visionary forms dramatic
which bright

Redounded from their Tongues in thunderous majesty, in
    Visions
In new Expanses, creating exemplars of Memory and of
    Intellect
Creating Space, Creating Time according to the wonders
    Divine
Of Human Imagination...[31]

Sam Shepard, the American playwright, made an interesting response to a questioner who asked where he got ideas for his plays. "Plays," he said, "don't come from ideas; ideas come from plays." This exchange is a perfect exemplar of the quarrel of imagination and reason. When reason usurps the place of the imagination, imagination's best recourse is the reversal of his premises. This is exactly what Los (a representative of the Imagination in this world), does when he says, "I will not Reason & Compare: my business is to Create."[32] For reasoning and comparing are taken by Urizen to be not only the defining product of the human being, but the very structure of divinity, which he, in turn, takes upon himself. But Los knows that nothing, not even reason itself, was ever reasoned into being.

A response like Los's or Shepard's is always greeted by the unbalanced, warring Zoas with Olympian disdain on the one hand and delight on the other. That we so immediately recognize the opposing parties reveals the persistence of what Blake calls the fall of the Zoas into disunity or imbalance. In a word, "single vision" rules. It ruled society in Blake's day, and it rules in ours. For an artist, a creator, or a builder of Jerusalem, the initial task is to reverse the premises (of single vision) and free the other Zoas. For, though imagination and reason are allowed to be parts of the creative process, and though the existence of emotion is at least acknowledged, the part of sensation, or the physical is routinely minimized or denied. We ignore, or conceal, our bodily responses to one another, to the world and to art, as though to weep with joy were a sign of weakness, and to touch one another as easily as children were a sign of bad manners and naiveté. Instead, that is, of recognizing ourselves as physically intersecting with something really present, we're encouraged to "see ourselves" as observers, commentators, annotators, recorders, collectors, buyers, sellers – as anything but participants in, and necessary builders of, art.

That we continue to deny the significance (and even existence!) of our physical involvement in Blake's art is remarkable in light of his earnest and repeated exhortations to the contrary. *Milton*, for instance, closes with several Zoa-related heroic forms looking on as "the Human Harvest" is prepared. The "Wine-presses & Barns stand open;" and "All Animals upon the Earth, are prepard in all their strength / To go forth to the Great Harvest & Vintage of the Nations."[33] We may argue that exactly what action is here called for is not clear, but we certainly can't deny that real, not symbolic, action is called for. Performance is demanded, not acknowledgment. Nor is it limited to Englishmen, or Christians – *all mankind* is here charged to "go forth." Again, in *Jerusalem* we discover a call not simply to action, but to a collective construction:

> Is this thy soft Family-Love
> Thy cruel Patriarchal pride
> Planting thy Family alone
> Destroying all the World beside.

> A mans worst enemies are those
> Of his own house & family;
> And he who makes his law a curse
> By his own law shall surely die.

> In my Exchanges *every* Land
> Shall walk, & mine in every Land,
> *Mutual shall build* Jerusalem:
> Both heart in heart & hand in hand.[34]

We read this language as symbolic, or rhetorical because we find it so hard to believe that it might be anything else. How could we have anything to do with such building? Even if we thought some action might be taken, what would it have to do with art? Wouldn't it have to be political or social? No. Because Blake's art, from which all my notions or ideas have been – I hope reasonably – derived, is obviously and remarkably different from what we have been taught to expect of art. Specifically, it makes powerfully spiritual, mental, emotional, and corporeal, or sensational demands on its audience. And since Blake's first task is subverting reason in order to release the other Zoas from single vision's tyranny, what better way to begin than by subverting the notion that words are nothing more than abstract symbols of even more abstract ideas? Words are, in Blake, for all the efforts of his editors to deny and conceal it, corporeal presences. Unlike other poets, for instance, he is concerned as much with the physical space occupied on the paper by his words in relation to the designs and colors in and about them as he is with any abstract ideas they may be said to 'signify.'

Consider what happens when readers encounter facsimile editions of Blake's works. At first, they are struck by the oddness of Blake's designs; some are even fascinated by what they call his "mixed media" approach. But they soon complain that it's hard to read his text – and they much prefer to read the typescript. But, evidently, he didn't want it to be easily read. He sought instead, the uncertain, multi- and ambivalent, individual perception of the physical shapes of the letters, marks and words. He wanted, that is, exactly the experience we have in reading the handwriting of people we know: in it we find a record of far more than their ideas – far more, in many cases, than they are conscious of! And our reading of the script, of course, also reveals a great deal about us, for as Blake remarked: "As a man is, So he Sees."[35]

Blake's readers, like the readers of the journal/notebooks, aren't asked simply to *think* about the texts, or reason about them, they are required, with remarkable consistency to ATTEND to them. The happy *Songs of Innocence* are written with a "rural pen" and "water clear" not to be read, but that "Every child may joy to *hear*" them.[36] With the opening of the *Songs of Experience,* we are told to *"Hear* the voice of the Bard!" and "Turn away no more."[37] In *Milton,* we are admonished to "Mark well my words! they are of your eternal salvation."[38] And in *Jerusalem,* Blake tells us that "Every word and every letter is studied and put *into its fit place."*[39] Nor is attending to placement of every letter merely an aesthetic requirement; it is necessary for our salvation: "I know of *no other Christianity* and of no other Gospel *than the liberty both of body & mind to exercise* the Divine Arts of Imagination."[40] We are told, again and again, to *listen to* and to *mark* Blake's words; words that have been studied and *put into their fit places* because we ourselves have been, likewise, studied and placed. For, as he reminds us, we are here to create, not to annotate:

> Can you think at all & not pronounce heartily! That to Labour in Knowledge. is to Build up Jerusalem: and to Despise Knowledge, is to Despise Jerusalem and her Builders.... Let every Christian as much as in him lies engage himself openly & publicly before all the World in some Mental pursuit for the Building up of Jerusalem[41]

"I do not seek, I find," Picasso famously tells us, pointing to the concrete locus of his work.[42] For art happens in the here and now; its materials are what is given. To look for the ideal insures that the looker will miss what is here to be found. Like Picasso's, Blake's art directs the viewer's attention to the physical – the actual – intersection of the work and his own life.[43] Architecture is the supremely practical art and the supremely participatory one as well, and it is by means of our participation, our knowing the mighty ones in us and in others, that we actually construct Jerusalem. Blake's goal, that is, is a particularly well-chosen one, for like the architect who works in volume and plane, acoustics & light, to build a habitation for the traveler through this world of time and space, Blake wishes us to construct from the light and line of his plates and from the pitch and timbre of his singing words, and from the harmony of their marriage in our lives and voices, an actual resting place for the pilgrim to and from Eternity, a testing place of the marriage of Heaven & Hell. Each of us is a member of this Holy city, for as the Four Zoas are in each of us, so are we, collectively, in each of them. In our action is found the universal brotherhood of Eden, without which there is no perfect unity.[44]

Contrary to the notion that Blake's art involves the participation of us all, editors, scholars and teachers seem resigned to its inaccessibility. Bentley's is a fair statement of this prevailing opinion: "Blake's works," he writes, "are so idiosyncratic, so much of the meaning comes through minutiae not only of coloring and design but of letter-formation and layout, that access to originals is of the first importance to anyone seriously concerned with what Blake meant."[45] Lacking access to these originals, a student has no choice but to rely on the opinions and judgments of those who have such access: wealthy collectors and those who can travel to several widely scattered libraries and museums. Such a situation seems almost bizarre enough to have come from Blake's own imagination! But is it true? Is Blake's art, finally, out of our reach? Or is it as close as the palm of your hand?

I remember hearing Martín Prechtel, a Guatemalan shaman, recount the *Popul Vuh*, the epic of the Maya. He prefaced his performance (which took about eight hours spaced over several mornings) by telling us that the *Popul Vuh* is not what has been told to, and written down by, the anthropologists. The reason is not simple hostility to scientists, but that the song belongs only to its singers, and each member of the village is responsible for part of the singing. When the epic needs to be reenacted, the entire population is involved – and the telling takes many days. But even if that performance were recorded, the result wouldn't be the *Popul Vuh*, for the song depends for its realization on the living moment shared by teller and told – and no single instance can contain the whole that is the *Popul Vuh*.[46] What we were about to hear, then, was not THE *Popul Vuh*, but OUR *Popul Vuh* – and precisely because it was ours, it could neither be entirely transmitted to, or wholly understood by, others. For Blake, too, the limit of the song is the range of the voice. Our access to him, then, is both as limited – and as open – as our access to the *Popul Vuh*.

We begin, then, by understanding something every student of Blake, sooner or later, realizes: the Blake that matters is *not* the Blake in the book. Indeed, the assumption that Blake's works are *books,* only different from other books in the peculiar nature of their manufacture and format, is the same as the one which assumes that a performance of the *Popul Vuh* is only different from a performance of *Hamlet* in the details of its setting. For the essence of the book as we understand and experience it is mass produced uniformity.[47] Likewise, literary scholars ordinarily think of individual works in terms of their fulfillment or subversion of generic constraints, and their location in the history of that genre. But the sources for Blake's works are, as he says, "in Eternity," and what they owe to the accident of his time and place are what, in his view, is least valuable about them. "The human mind," he wrote, "cannot go beyond the gift of God, the Holy Ghost. To suppose that Art can go beyond the finest specimens of Art that are now in the world, is not knowing what Art is; it is being blind to the gifts of the spirit."[48] Works of art, that is, are realizations in the moment – and with the aid of the Zoas – of the gift of the Holy Spirit. The artist labors to realize the gift, not to fulfill or subvert the genre, exactly as Jesus, in Blake's great vision that opens Chapter Four of *Jerusalem*, contends with the Wheel of Religion, neither subverting nor fulfilling it, but, instead, "Creating Nature" from it, by "self-denial & forgiveness of Sin."[49]

The Marriage of Heaven and Hell contains five unusual, first person narratives Blake calls "Memorable Fancies." The probable origin of this unusual label – and Blake's title itself – is Emmanuel Swedenborg, whose *Heaven and Hell* is among those works annotated by Blake which have survived.[50] In it, Swedenborg called accounts of his visionary adventures, "memorable relations." *The Marriage of Heaven and Hell* – and the Memorable Fancies in it – are, however, entirely unlike their "source." In fact, they are unlike anything, anywhere.[51] Harold Bloom calls them "parodies" of Swedenborg's "relations," but that term is inadequate, suggesting, as it does, burlesque and ridicule which are remote both from Blake's evident intent and his effect on the reader. Bloom also claims a satirical purpose for the entire work, naming Rabelais as the "intellectual satirist closest in his vision" to Blake.[52] The usefulness of such formal classification, even when the thing classified doesn't fit, is, presumably, that it removes doubt and resolves unsettling questions. But that Blake sees such abstract classifying as not only foolish, but actually malignant may be seen in the opening lines of *The Marriage of Heaven and Hell:*

> Once meek, and in a perilous path,
> The just man kept his course along
> The vale of death.
>
> …
>
> Till the villain left the paths of ease,
> To walk in perilous paths, and drive
> The just man into barren climes.
>
> Now the sneaking serpent walks

In mild humility.
And the just man rages in the wilds
Where lions roam.[53]

He turns from this lyrical condemnation of hypocrisy to an explicit rejection of Swedenborg's and Milton's systematic classifications of Good and Evil in Christianity – not only because they are classifications, but also because they pretend to remove doubt and death from the just man's path and to settle for him the difficulties of scripture.[54] It is no surprise that Blake is hostile to any system offering universal answers – and especially to those who offer easy ones! His criticism here may be sarcastic, but it is not satirical. The artist's choices, like the just man's, are always specific, never general. Likewise, his models.

"Greek or Roman Models," remember, are not required, "if we are but just & true to our own Imaginations."[55] Blake repeatedly and explicitly rejects the notion that a work of art can have anything other than its own distinct and uniquely original form. "Ideas cannot be Given but in their minutely Appropriate Words nor Can a Design be made without its minutely Appropriate Execution."[56] And again: "General Knowledge is Remote Knowledge it is in Particulars that Wisdom consists & Happiness too. Both in Art & in Life General Masses are as much Art as a Pasteboard Man is Human ... but he who enters into and discriminates most minutely ... is the alone Wise or Sensible Man & on this discrimination All Art is founded."[57] All true art is founded on, that is, on specificity.[58] And art, as we have seen, in Blake is not entertainment or instruction, but salvation. Individual participation in particular detail can't be reduced to rule or, in the conventional sense, taught. The conventions of classification made possible by abstract thought are, then, the enemies, not the sources, of art, for they become ideals against which individual works are judged – and found wanting.

Since, for Blake, the source of art was the same as the source of life itself, a generic consideration was no less than a triple blasphemy: against God, man and art. It is, he writes, the basis of his opposition to the (neoclassical) art of his day and the reason, incidentally, that his own work is undervalued: "Reynoldss [sic] Opinion was that Genius May be Taught & that all Pretence to Inspiration is a Lie & a Deceit to say the least of it…For if it is a Deceit the whole Bible is Madness This Opinion originates in the Greeks Calling the Muses Daughters of Memory…The Enquiry in England is not whether a Man has Talents. & Genius? But whether he is Passive & Polite & a Virtuous Ass: & obedient to Noblemens Opinions in Art & Science. If he is; he is a Good Man: If Not he must be Starvd"[59]

Over against the established rational theory of art and its relation to nature, Blake set what we would call a notion of organic form, but which he labeled "Gothic."[60] His choice of the word (which in his time meant "barbaric"), was as much for its association with his visionary Christianity as for his appreciation of the individual felicities and spiritual harmonies of the monuments in which he had received much of his original training in drawing. The distinction between these two, fundamentally opposed, ways of thinking about art and reality was so crucial to his life and art that he made an attack on Classical art the subject of a single etched plate. The concluding words are arranged there as follows:

> Rome and Greece swept Art into their maw & destroyd it
> a Warlike State never can produce Art. It will Rob & Plunder
> & accumulate into one place. & Translate & Copy & Buy &
> Sell & Criticise. but not Make. Grecian is Mathematic Form
> Mathematic Form is Eternal in   Gothic is Living
> The Reasoning Memory. Living   Form.
> is Eternal Existence[61]

To the artists of his day who, like Sir Joshua Reynolds, looked to "Nature," or the physical world, as a reasonable and scientific source of their art, Blake responded with scorn.[62] For as he understands the necessity of looking through, rather than with, his eyes, so he also understands that the models for his art are not any more to be found in the physical world than they are in the plaster casts of the academy. "No Man of Sense can think that an Imitation of the Objects of Nature is The Art of Painting or that such Imitation which any one may easily perform is worthy of Notice," he wrote impatiently in his notes for a proposed address to the public.[63] And in "A Descriptive Catalogue," similarly addressed to the public (it accompanied a showing of his work in 1809 at his brother's shop in Golden Square), he precisely specified the source of his work – and how he labors to capture it:

> The connoisseurs and artists who have made objections to Mr. B.'s mode of representing spirits with real bodies, would do well to consider that the Venus, the Minerva, the Jupiter, the Apollo, which they admire in Greek statues, are all of them representations of spiritual existences of God's immortal, [invisible] to the mortal perishing organ of sight; and yet they are embodied and organized in solid marble. Mr. B. requires the same latitude and all is well. The Prophets describe what they saw in Vision as real and existing men whom they saw with their imaginative and immortal organs; the Apostles the same; the clearer the organ the more distinct the object. A Spirit and a Vision are not, as the modern philosophy supposes, a cloudy vapour or a nothing: they are organized and minutely articulated beyond all that the mortal and perishing nature can produce. *He who does not imagine in stronger and better lineaments, and in stronger and better light than his perishing mortal eye can see does not imagine at all.* The painter of this work asserts that all his imaginations appear to him infinitely more perfect and more minutely organized than any thing seen by his mortal eye.[64]

We see here that Blake was perfectly aware of what we call material reality. And he was even clearer about the growing shift in his contemporaries' attitudes towards art and religion. There is a growing sense of art as commodity, a source of pleasure or edification,[65] and of religion as a social phenomenon with origins in primitive superstition. Most of his fellow citizens have uncritically accepted the modern division of experience into solid empirical fact on the one hand, and vague, inessential fictions like "soul," "truth," and "beauty" on the other. Yet even today, after the triumph of science, no one has a better sense than Blake of the basis of reality in an energy of indescribable scope and inexhaustible supply.[66] And if he is (sometimes painfully) aware of the existence of material reality, he also knows its value: "When a young musician visited him ... he told him 'he had a palace of his own of great beauty and magnificence. On Mr Rundall's looking round the room for evidence, Blake remarked, 'You don't think I am such a fool as to think this is it.'"[67]

No one is plainer than Blake about the faculty of imaginative vision. There is nothing of the obscurantist in him, for he held that he shared fourfold vision, as he shared the Four Zoas, with all men: "Of the faculty of Vision he spoke as One he had had from early infancy – He thinks all men partake of it – but it is lost by not being cultivated. And he eagerly assented to a remark I made that all men have all faculties to a greater or less degree."[68] And so, when I assign my students the task of creating a "Memorable Fancy," I look forward to their requests for more detail. You have five Memorable Fancies to look to for pointers, I say, and you know as well what they are as any other soul. Blake doesn't believe in genre and abstract rules, but in concrete and detailed eternal reality. Knowing, as you now do, from your journal/notebooks and your Illuminations, that your audience consists in all the members of the seminar, not simply the teacher, and knowing further that, until you struggle with the work of saying it, that is, of minutely organizing it in all its particulars, neither you, nor anyone in the world, *can* know it,[69] you are free to undertake what Dylan Thomas calls, "the most rewarding work in the world." For, as he wrote, and as Blake would agree: "A good poem is a contribution to reality. The world is never the same once a good poem has been added to it. A good poem helps to change the shape and significance of the universe, helps to extend everyone's knowledge of himself and of the world around him."[70] In our context, "poem" here means a work of the imagination or fourfold vision, not a literary composition in verse. I look forward, then, to your own "organized and minutely articulated visions."

In the end, Blake's work belongs, that is, not to the collectors or the scholars but to those who are carrying on the work he began and who understand that that work is what they surrender to the building of Jerusalem, not what they claim, or buy, or sell, or collect, or otherwise withhold. Because all that anyone has to contribute of value, of his own unique and individual vision, finds that value only by joining in the divine structure Blake calls Jerusalem. His work, like ours, does not constitute Jerusalem, is not itself, reality, but is indeed a contribution to it – and not for its own sake, but for the sake of all. In this light, the

following words, which he added to his engraving of the *Laocoön*, glow
as brilliantly as the faces of newborn children:

> There are States in which all Visionary Men are accounted
>   Mad Men   such are Greece & Rome   Such is
>   Empire or Tax
> Art Degraded Imagination Denied War Governd the Nations
> Divine Union Deriding And Denying Immediate Communion
>   with God
> The Spoilers say Where are his Works That he did in the
>   Wilderness
> …
>
> Prayer is the Study of Art
> Praise is the Practice of Art
> …
>
> The outward Ceremony is Antichrist
> Without Unceasing Practise nothing can be done
> Practice is Art   If you leave off you are Lost[71]

Probably the lines of Blake most quoted, even more often than
the opening of "The Tyger" are these, from a Notebook poem called
"Auguries of Innocence":

> To see a World in a Grain of Sand
> And a Heaven in a Wild Flower
> Hold Infinity in the palm of your hand
> And Eternity in an hour[72]

A course in Blake, as Deb Agaard wrote one day in her journal/note-
book, is one informed by an awareness that what we all must do – and
all the time – is "work toward knowing." And the importance of that
work may be measured by considering that, although these are the
most widely quoted lines of Blake, they are, at the same time, almost
completely unheard and unheeded. For they are not a pleasing sound,
or an edifying instruction. They are *explicit and practical directions* for the

exercise of our imaginative and immortal organs of vision. The operative word, here, is "hold." To see, it is essential that we find in ourselves and in one another, the Four Zoas. But before we start, and while we continue on, we must find, and *hold,* our balance.

free from danger

Three: That Immortal Sound

O that men would seek immortal moments
O that men would converse with God

WILLIAM BLAKE, "Annot. Lavater"

According to John Thomas Smith (1766-
1833), Blake, on the day of his death, "composed and uttered songs to
his Maker so sweetly to the ear of his Catherine, that when she stood to
hear him, he, looking upon her most affectionately, said, 'My beloved,
they are not mine – no – they are not mine.'"[1] It isn't known who, other
than Catherine, heard these songs, but all the contemporary accounts
of his death mention them.[2] And it would have been strange had he
left this life any other way for, not only did he consider death no more
than "removing from one room to another,"[3] but he'd heard such sweet
music all his life, including one time in his teens, when he found himself alone in West Minster Abbey and suddenly, "The aisles and gal-
leries of the old building (or sanctuary)…filled with a great procession
of monks and priests, choristers and censer-bearers, and his entranced
ear heard the chant of plain-song and chorale, while the vaulted roof
trembled to the sound of organ music."[4] Not only did he hear these
melodies, he also shared them with friends and companions. Smith,
who called William's younger brother, Robert, one of his 'playfellows,'
remembers going to an artistic gathering at the Mathew's house in

Rathbone Place in the 1780's: "At that lady's [Mrs. Mathew's] most agreeable conversaziones [sic] I first met William Blake, the artist.... There have I often heard him read and sing several of his poems. He was listened to by the company with profound silence, and allowed by most visitors to possess original and extraordinary merit."[5] According to Smith, Blake's remarkable musical gift was entirely owed to natural talent, for, "though, according to his confession, he was entirely unacquainted with the science of music, his ear was so good, that his tunes were sometimes most singularly beautiful, and were noted down by musical professors."[6]

Alexander Gilchrist attests both to Blake's love of music and to his continuing the practice of spontaneous composition and singing well into his later years. He writes of the old man's visits to the Linnell house in Hampstead Heath where, "He was very fond of hearing Mrs. Linnell sing Scottish songs, and would sit by the pianoforte, tears falling from his eyes, while he listened...To simple...melodies Blake was very impressionable, though not so to music of more complicated structure. He himself still sang, in a voice tremulous with age, sometimes old ballads, sometimes his own songs, to melodies of his own."[7] Nor was his singing limited to leisure moments. According to Allan Cunningham's memoir, published three years after Blake's death, "In sketching designs, engraving plates, writing songs, and composing music, he employed his time, with his wife sitting at his side, encouraging him in all his undertakings. As he drew the figure he meditated the song which was to accompany it, and the music to which the verse was to be sung, was the offspring too of the same moment. Of his music there are no specimens – he wanted the art of noting it down – if it equaled many of his drawings, and some of his songs, we have lost melodies of real value."[8]

Though he wanted the art of musical notation, Blake had, "a natural aptitude for acquiring knowledge, [and] ...was always willing to apply himself to the vocabulary of a language for the purpose of reading a great original author. He would declare that he learnt French, sufficient to read it, in a few weeks. By-and-by, at sixty years of age, he will set to learning Italian, in order to read Dante."[9] It's fair to say that if he thought musical notation necessary, it would have been easy for him to acquire it. But since the melodies were, as he said, "not his" and were truly offspring of the moment, it is difficult to see why they should have been recorded. In short, if anything has been "lost," it is our belief in the significance of the moment – and in the value of our own voices in it!

And anyway, there are other ways of learning (and keeping[10]) music than notation. When you learn the words to a song, you learn a melody too. And a song that is so remembered – as were the 'simpler' tunes so loved of Blake – is made new each time it is sung: its mood and tempo, even its melody and words; all are suited to the singer, the moment, and the audience. This is the method of the bard, or ballad singer, and it is an exact correlative to Blake's other remarkable lifetime practice: that of never illuminating an individual plate, or of assembling and finishing an individual volume, in the same manner or to the same end. Each is an individual performance: born, celebrating – and dying – in the moment. Still, there are always those who try to hold it and, failing, turn away in sorrow:

> Ah! Thel is like a watry bow. and like a parting cloud.
> Like a reflection in a glass. like shadows in the water.
> Like dreams of infants. like a smile upon an infants face,
> Like the doves voice, like transient day, like music in the air[11]

Trapped in the logic of time and space, Thel wants to replace the gift of the moment with something unchanging and permanent, something perfect. But Eternity, as Blake saw, is discovered not in the made, but in the making.

We find and keep his melodies (though he knew they were not really his), in the same way he illuminated his designs: by holding infinity in the palm of our hand; by taking ourselves, in the moment, to "the source," that is: the Poetic Genius.[12] Blake sang through his death, as he sang through his life: spontaneously. By deliberately placing ("fitting") his words wholly in the moment of their utterance, balancing singer, song, and audience, he marked, rather than recorded, them.[13] He left us, then, what pianist Keith Jarrett calls, "the fragile (and at times distant) knowledge that music is in the making of the music. The heart is where the music is."[14]

In *VISIONS of the Daughters of Albion*, Blake refutes the systematic reduction of experience to notation. In it, Oothoon, a mysterious female – whose name almost requires our singing, not saying, it – laments her rape by the God-tormented[15] agents of perfection:

> They told me that the night & day were all that I could see;
> They told me that I had five senses to inclose me up.
> And they inclos'd my infinite brain into a narrow circle.
> And sunk my heart into the Abyss, a red, round globe hot
>   burning
> Till all from life I was obliterated and erased.[16]

By asserting the exclusive reality of single vision and perfection, they reject the infinite resonance of the actual moment and claim an either/or status for guilt and innocence. But Oothoon, like us all, is both guilty *and* innocent. And when, like Blake, she listens, she can hear another voice. For, as Walter Lowrie puts it so eloquently,

> Process or becoming is the key to the human being, who
> exists not as a creature – something either flawed or finished –
> but as a respondent to God's call, the being who hears. She
> is, in process of becoming, she is constantly striving, and this
> movement is prompted by passion – that is, by imagination
> and feeling, rather than by thinking. All these traits are existential because they eventuate in a transformation of…
> existence.[17]

It was, perhaps, Blake's "unschooled" willingness to seize every moment and every opportunity that came to hand which accounts for the (to many) baffling and agonizing tendency of his work to be derived from what seems to be accidental. The *Songs of Innocence and of Experience,* for instance, seem to have their origin in children's illustrated books; *The Marriage of Heaven and Hell* to be derived from Swedenborg; the *Book of Urizen,* to owe as much to the accident of the numbering of Bible verses and the double column printing of contemporary publishers as to the idea of subverting or inverting Genesis; *Vala* seems to grow awkwardly out of Young's tiresome *Night Thoughts,* only gradually permitting Blake's own structure to emerge as *The Four*

Zoas; and, finally, seemingly incidental details of Blake's biography are incorporated into the action and myth of *Milton* and *Jerusalem.* But, from Blake's standpoint, it is in the grasping of the moment that art actually lives, even as it is in its coherence and logic that *Paradise Lost* is most misleading and dangerous. For it sets Creation, Incarnation and the Judgment, ever present realities, at an infinite and eternal, remove. As the Zoa diagram from *Milton* shows, Milton's descent from that (false) perfection into the balance of the Four Mighty Ones in the (eternal) moment generates the "Divine Revelation," wherein "Jesus wept & walked forth / From Felpham's Vale…& the Four surrounded him." Even more interestingly, it is an "immortal sound" which triggers Blake's recognition:

> Terror struck in the Vale I stood at *that immortal sound*
> My bones trembled. I fell outstretchd upon the path
> A *moment*, & my Soul returnd into its mortal state
> To Resurrection & Judgment in the Vegetable Body
> And my sweet Shadow of Delight stood trembling by my side[18]

If the moment of resurrection and judgment – standing, falling, and rising again in the body – is to take place really and eternally, when other than now, where other than here, where each of us stands with a sweet shadow of delight trembling at our side?

Blake's works, then, deliberately defy categorization; his texts are not merely words, but (ever elusive and always present) notes; his designs are not mere representations, but illuminations of the moment. The reason lies not in the artist's ignorance, but in his intent, for his works are visions, not of nature or society, but of eternity. "Manners make the Man, not Habits." he writes in his Notebook, "It is the same in Art by their Works ye shall know them."[19] In a word, it is art's catalytic effect which counts, not its category; what is created by the pattern of a life, moment by specific moment, is what matters, not the labels (good and evil, orthodox and heretical) attached after the fact. For Blake, the artist is, like Christ, an agent of liberation, not of definition. And so he reckons good and evil not in categorical terms but in active ones: good is active, evil is restraint:

> The Philosophy of Causes & Consequences misled Lavater
> as it has all his contemporaries. Each thing is its own cause &
> its own effect. Accident is the omission of act in self & the
> hindering of act in another. This is Vice, but all Act from
> Individual propensity is Virtue. To hinder another is not an
> act; it is the contrary; it is a restraint on action both in our-
> selves & in the person hindered, for he who hinders another
> omits his own duty at the time. Murder is hindering another.
> Theft is hindering another. Backbiting, Undermining,
> Circumventing & whatever is Negative is Vice. But the origin
> of this mistake in Lavater & his contemporaries, is, They sup-
> pose that Woman's Love is Sin; in consequence all the Loves
> & Graces with them are Sin.[20]

The artist and the Christian, then, are the woman or man whose
work liberates its audience and moves them to act "from (their own)
Individual propensity." The artist's work is a gift, with a gift's obligation, not a commodity for trading. As a gift, it asks its audience's participation, not merely their reception. As the relation of performer and
audience is participatory, so that of art and viewer is sacramental, not
mercantile; we are celebrants, not producer and consumer.[21] Hence
Blake's disgust with Commerce and advertising in art and society:
"Suffer not the fashionable Fools to depress your powers by the prices
they pretend to give for contemptible works or the expensive advertiz-
ing boasts that they make of such works; believe Christ & his Apostles
that there is a Class of Men whose whole delight is in Destroying."[22]

Because he lived in a time when, as he saw it, the art world was
cooperating in its own destruction by making nature its source and
profit its goal, he told Henry Crabb Robinson: "I should be sorry if I
had any earthly fame, for whatever natural glory a man has, so much is
detracted from his spiritual glory. I wish to do nothing for profit. I wish
to live for art."[23] Using what is given by the moment and bringing to it
all his faculties – sensual and emotive, as well as rational and intuitive
– Blake lived for art and left us a number of priceless gifts, which are,
like Schubert's *lieder*, contributions to reality, not descriptions of it. For
they are, as he repeatedly asserted, visions of Eternity. Not *the* vision of
Eternity, a complete and finished thing, but the spontaneous glimpses

of one member of Jerusalem, a man who spent his time building that Holy City and who, at the end of his life, cheerfully sang his way into it.

But what about us? Removed from the sound of his voice, and lacking the cheerful confidence of his presence, with no more than the silent traces of his gift, we face the immediate problem of "reading," or somehow grasping his prophetic books. Never mind building or entering Jerusalem, the confused reader exclaims, how am I supposed to *locate* myself in the tumbling confusion of these pages? Who are these readers, or "Public," addressed at the opening of *Jerusalem:* "After my three years slumber on the banks of the Ocean, I again display my Giant forms to the Public: My former Giants & Fairies having reciev'd the highest reward possible: the love and friendship of those with whom to be connected is to be blessed: I cannot doubt that this more consolidated & extended Work will be as kindly recieved."[24] Are these "blessed" souls the "Sheep" and we, confused and incapable of receiving his Giant Forms, the "Goats," making up the division Blake etched at the top of the page, presumably at the same time that he mysteriously mutilated it?[25] Again, knowing from *The Marriage of Heaven and Hell* that Blake delights in inverting categories, how can we be sure that the Goats – ourselves – are not, in fact, the blessed ones? All that seems certain is our confusion, hesitation and weariness, for, as Jerome McGann has remarked: "Reading Blake is a physically demanding task, as everyone knows who has confronted what have aptly been called those 'walls of words' on the plates, especially in *Milton* and *Jerusalem*."[26] And even if we have accepted the proposition that meaning, in Blake, somehow emerges from the interaction of text and design, how are we to deal with the minute but mysterious detail in the designs and the accumulated weight of verses packed in all around them?

For it is one thing to manage the brief narratives of *The Marriage of Heaven and Hell* or *The Book of Thel* and the individual lyrics of *Songs of Innocence and of Experience,* but it is quite another to struggle with the density of *Milton* and *Jerusalem!* And Blake's contemporaries were as baffled by them as we are. The notion that the music of Blake's verse decayed from an early "natural sweetness" to a fanatical harshness began as early as Robert Southey's dismissal of *Jerusalem* as a "perfectly mad" poem.[27] It continued with Crabb Robinson's dismissal of the prophecies, which he was only able to say "appeared to be" in verse.[28] In 1806 Benjamin Heath Malkin attempted to put Blake's efforts in the best possible light by suggesting that he was at least in earnest, though out of step with the times:

> He has made several irregular and unfinished attempts at po-
> etry. He has dared to venture on the ancient simplicity; and
> feeling it in his own character and manners, has succeeded
> better than those, who have only seen it through a glass. His
> genius in this line assimilates more with the bold and careless
> freedom, peculiar to our writers at the latter end of the six-
> teenth, and former part of the seventeenth century, than
> with the polished phraseology, and just, but subdued thought
> of the eighteenth.[29]

However much Malkin approved of Blake's lyrics, writing that in them, "words and numbers present themselves unbidden, when the soul is inspired by sentiment, elevated by enthusiasm, or ravished by devotion," his final judgment on the prophecies is that neither Blake's evident devotion nor his enthusiasm could offset the "unrestrained measure" of the prophetic books, which "betrayed him into so wild a pursuit of fancy, as to leave harmony unregarded, and to pass the line prescribed by criticism to the career of the imagination."[30] Gilchrist agreed that Blake's verse decayed with his advancing age, and added that (with a few exceptions), so too, did his designs:

> After the *Songs of Experience,* Blake never again sang to like
> angelic tunes; nor even with the same approach to technical
> accuracy. His poetry was the blossom of youth and early man-
> hood. Neither in design did he improve on the tender grace of
> some of these illustrations; irregularities became as conspicu-
> ous in it, as in his verse; though in age he attained to nobler
> heights of sublimity, as the Inventions to Job will exemplify.[31]

He attributes this failure to, "the occasional tendency to vagueness of motive, to an expression of abstract emotions, more legitimate for the sister art of music than for poetry, which must be definite, however deep and subtle. The tendency grew in Blake's after writings and over-mastered him."[32]

Modern critics, though generally more friendly to Blake, are often either exculpatory or evasive about the prophetic books. Though Mona Wilson, for instance, credits the poet's dedication and energy, and makes a detailed survey of his evolving metrics, she concludes that, "The form of the symbolic books is…a stumbling block. The poet who had been so bold and felicitous in his prosodic innovations never entirely lost his lyrical gift," but in the end his, "obscure mythology and inharmonious prosody bar the access to the symbolic books. At a first reading they will appear to most people – and many would never approach them but for their illuminated printing – a smouldering rubbish heap, dimly lit by flickering flames of sense and beauty, but the heap will seem so large and the little flames so rare that most of them will pass it by."[33]

Though F.R. Leavis unequivocally dismisses the prophetic books as failures,[34] he is correct about their intent. They are, he writes, intended to bring about, "the restoration of the Eternal Man."[35] And, again, he is refreshingly direct about what he describes as the evidence of that failure. He finds that, "For us, of course, it isn't the supreme reality attained at last, the really real: it is a plunge into wordy and boring unreality."[36] Leavis, in other words, only differs from the rest of us in the bluntness of his description of his experience of confronting Blake's prophecies. Like us, he's unsure whether or not he is among the goats or sheep, and somewhat put out, I think, about Blake's apparent indifference to his predicament!

But is the restoration of the Eternal Man, the holding of infinity in the palm of one's hand, a simple task? Can, or should, it be? Blake didn't think so. The Preface to *Milton* and the prose addresses in *Jerusalem* attest to his awareness that he had to prepare his readers. The principal difficulty, as he sees it, rises from our habits of mind and approaches to art and reality, habits and attitudes he worked tirelessly throughout his life to overthrow. In 1799, for instance, he had occasion to deal with the Rev. Dr. Trusler's disappointment with some watercolors the Rev. had commissioned from him. Fortunately, Trusler kept Blake's reply, though it hardly presents him in a flattering light.[37] Evidently Trusler's expectations for Blake's pictures were rather

similar to Leavis' and our (unstated) requirements for a successful work
of art: in a word, that it meet some more or less consistent canons of
excellence and bear, in some comprehensible way, on 'reality' as we
conceive it.

Blake begins his response by establishing that his understanding
of the commission was that what had been requested of him was a
"Moral Painting." He's sorry to find Trusler disappointed with his efforts, but adds, "If I am wrong I am wrong in good company. I had
hoped your plan comprehended All Species of this Art & Especially
that you would not reject that Species which gives Existence to Every
other. namely Visions of Eternity."[38] His remarks, that is, are directed
less at Trusler's objections to his execution of the commission than to
his misunderstanding of the nature of Moral Painting. In that sense
the letter can serve as a response to all of us who find our expectations
disappointed in our encounter with his art. In effect, he is saying, 'If
you ask me for a sample of my vision, you mustn't expect the results
to mirror, or confirm, your own.' His rejection of what we might call
philosophical verisimilitude can, in fact, be taken as anticipating much
of what modern painters have been at pains to establish:

> I know that This World Is a World of Imagination & Vision
> I see Every thing I paint In This World, but Every body does
> not see alike. To the Eyes of a Miser a Guinea is more beau-
> tiful than the Sun & a bag worn with the use of Money has
> more beautiful proportions than a Vine filled with Grapes.
> The tree which moves some to tears of joy is in the Eyes of
> others only a Green thing that stands in the way. Some See
> Nature all Ridicule & Deformity & by these I shall not regu-
> late my proportions, & Some Scarce see Nature at all But to
> the Eyes of a Man of Imagination Nature is Imagination itself
> As a man is So he Sees.[39]

For Blake, art is addressed not to our reasoning faculty, but to
our imaginative one. This is why, he continues, the Bible is "more
Entertaining & Instructive than any other book...[because it]..."is addressed to the Imagination which is Spiritual Sensation & but mediately
to the Understanding or Reason."[40] And because his art is addressed

to the Imagination, it is, he says in the kind of remark that leaves the theologians and philosophers gasping like fish out of water, as easily grasped and understood by its intended audience as is the Bible: "I am happy to find a Great Majority of Fellow Mortals who can Elucidate my Visions & Particularly they have been Elucidated by Children."[41]

The part in us which finds Blake wordy and boring, then, is not the Imagination. The imagination (especially the child's) is *immediately* enabled by art; its participation, in turn, elucidates (that is, throws light on) the work – and the individual's relation to it. The process is dynamic, cumulative and non-divisible.[42] For the work by itself is dark, but when it is joined to the imagination of the spectator/audience, they are mutually illuminated. There is a world of difference between interpretation, (a matter of rules and grammars, of principles and abstractions), and elucidation or illumination (a matter of tempo and rhythm, intuition and sensation).[43]

What we experience as boredom and wordiness comes from our bringing to Blake the expectation that art is a kind of intellectual exercise, a game of self (or collective)-expression, or a manipulation and/or subversion of conventions. This complacent condescension to the imagination infuriates Blake; the notebooks, poems, and letters brim with his anger at those who would turn art into a matter of fashion or commerce, and forget or deny its eternal source and ecstatic end. For Blake, the poem or painting cannot exist independently of its source or its elucidation. The composite nature of his art, the method of its production, the life of the artist – even his dying words – all bear witness to the stringent demands of his art, both on him and his audience.[44] These demands are made explicit in *Milton*, when the great poet lists them as reasons for his descent to, and joining with, Blake:

> I come in Self-annihilation & the grandeur of Inspiration
> To cast off Rational Demonstration by Faith in the Saviour
> To cast off the rotten rags of Memory by Inspiration
>
> To cast off Bacon, Locke & Newton from Albions covering
> To take off his filthy garments, & clothe him with Imagination
> To cast aside from Poetry, all that is not Inspiration

> That it no longer shall dare to mock with the aspersion of
>   Madness
> Cast on the Inspired, by the tame high finishers of paltry
>   Blots,
>
> Indefinite, or paltry Rhymes; or paltry Harmonies.[45]

The demands of his art on its audience are also specified in his Notebook draft of an essay intended to accompany a showing of a painting of "The Last Judgment:"

> If the Spectator could Enter into these Images in his
> Imagination, approaching them on the Fiery Chariot of his
> Contemplative Thought; if he could Enter into Noah's
> Rainbow, or into his bosom; or could make a Friend & Com-
> panion of one of these Images of wonder – which always en-
> treats him to leave mortal things as he must know…then
> would he meet the Lord in the Air & then he would be
> happy…. Every Man has Eyes, Nose, & Mouth. This every
> Idiot knows; but he who enters into & discriminates most mi-
> nutely…is the alone Wise or Sensible Man…. I entreat then,
> that the Spectator will attend to the Hands & Feet, to the
> Lineaments of the Countenences; they are all descriptive of
> Character & not a line is drawn without intention & that
> most discriminate & particular. As Poetry admits not a Letter
> that is Insignificant, so Painting admits not a Grain of Sand
> or a Blade of Grass Insignificant, much less an insignificant
> Blur or Mark.[46]

This emphasis on discrimination and attention to the smallest de-tail removes any thought that what Blake means by the exercise of the imagination is passive swooning or enthusiastic gushing. Indeed, Blake understood, better than most, that the true artist and scientist is the one paying the most careful attention to the details, even as the good shepherd is he that knows each of his sheep as he himself is known, *individually*.[47] If we are 'wise and sensible' then, we labor with the art-ist 'in eternity' for the restoration of the Eternal One (for, that is, the salvation of each *individual* soul). And this begins deeply inside us, with the individual sound of our own voice making, here and now, the music of Blake's verses.

Again, he has anticipated our difficulty with his verse, most famously in his prefatory remarks, "Of the Measure, in which the following Poem is written," in *Jerusalem*. But, in striking contrast to Milton's note on the verse of *Paradise Lost*, which relates it to the epic poems of Homer and Milton,[48] Blake begins: "We who dwell on Earth can do nothing of ourselves, every thing is conducted by Spirits, no less than Digestion or Sleep To Note the last words of Jesus, 'All power is given unto me in heaven and in earth.'"[49] That is to say, the sound of the following poem is determined – like every other thing we do in our lives – not by the precepts of the classical poets, or the scholars and grammarians, but by Jesus. When we recall that, for Blake, Jesus is both the prophet of the New Testament *and* "The Family Divine as One Man;" that he is co-extensive with "our own Imaginations, those Worlds of Eternity in which we shall live for ever; in [Him],"[50] these opening words can be understood to pertain directly to the matter of our reading – and sounding – of the following poem. For it is not a task that we undertake alone. In fact, as is stated later in *Jerusalem:*

> He who would see the Divinity must see him in his Children
> One first, in friendship & love; then a Divine Family, & in the
>   midst
> Jesus will appear; so he who wishes to see a Vision, a perfect
>   Whole
> Must see it in its Minute Particulars; Organized[51]

In a word, we can't read the poem alone – and it is our misguided notion that we can (even as we are permitted to imagine we alone determine all our actions), that so confuses us when we confront any of Blake's prophetic works. It is one with the notion that variation occurs within a set of rules or parameters (so loved of academics and other reasoners) and, thus, may be absorbed in a set of abstractions supposed (unlike the individual variant) to be perfect and eternal. Blake argues that this attitude towards individuality has its origins in socio/political thought, which, in turn, has economic causes & consequences.

Resigned as he is to dealing with those who have "eyes and see not,' and have 'ears and hear not,'[52] his ultimate appeal is not to our abstract reason, but to our actual, physical ears:

> The wretched State of the Arts in this Country & in Europe originating in the Wretched State of Political Science which is the Science of Sciences Demands a firm & determinate conduct on the part of Artists to Resist the Contemptible Counter Arts [which have been established by]…traders to the destruction of all true art…

> …An Example of these Contrary [or Counter] Arts is given us in the Characters of Milton & Dryden as they are written in a Poem signed with the name of Nat Lee which perhaps he never wrote & perhaps he wrote in a paroxysm of insanity In which it is said that Miltons Poem is a rough Unfinishd Piece & Dryden has finishd it Now let Drydens Fall & Miltons Paradise be read & I will assert that every Body of Understanding must cry out Shame on such a Niggling & Poco Piu as Dryden has degraded Milton with But at the same time I will allow that Stupidity will Prefer Dryden because it is in Rhyme & Monotonous Sing Song Sing Song from beginning to end[53]

It is significant that Blake calls not for us to "read" the two poems, but that they "be read," that is, that we *hear,* and then judge, them. The arts in Europe have sunk in Blake's estimation because the firm and determinate hand of the artist has been replaced with the cliché, that is, the sloppy, monotonous and predictable practice of the tradesman or commercial 'artist.' What is required for our reading of the prophetic works, on the other hand, is not theory or a meta-discourse,[54] but a community.

Fran Quinn, the poet, and I were talking one afternoon about the problem I was having trying to teach the reading of Blake's prophetic line, when he recalled an experience he had had some years back which, he thought, might be helpful. It seems that he had been asked to do a public performance of Whitman's "Out of the Cradle Endlessly

Rocking." As he was rehearsing this one hundred and eighty four line lyric, everything seemed to go well – until he got to line 173: "Death, death, death, death, death." Every time I got to this line, he said, I started laughing; I couldn't figure out what was wrong. Five monosyllables! What could be the problem? And yet every time, I had to laugh. So I was complaining to a friend of mine, an opera singer, and she insisted that I read the poem to her. And when I got the line she said, 'To get smoothly through that line, you have to make the tempo for the rest of the poem that prepares for it. That's why it's there.'

The tempo? I said, what do you mean? How fast you go? No. he said, it's not that mechanical. It's more like how it swings; it's like the walk you fall into unconsciously with your friend; so that when she stops to look at something, so do you. Naturally, and with no awkwardness. And you hold. And hold. And then, when she looks back at you, you move with her like you were dancing. And, in fact, you are. You're dancing with Whitman? I said. You've got it. He said, Now you've got it.

So, I said, how do we apply this to Blake? Will you come to my class and explain it? I'll come to your class, he said, but I won't explain it. So I told them to practice reading out loud to themselves and come to class ready to talk about what happened. And they did.

The first student, I think it was Barb Bishop, put up her hand and said, I can't even read the first line! So read it now, Fran says. So she reads: 'But Los, who is the Vehicular Form of strong Urthona.'[55] I'm thinking, meanwhile, to myself, Great! We're at line one and already we don't have any tempo! So much for that theory. Then Fran says, What comes before it? And Barb says, Nothing. It's the first line. Not in my book, says Fran. So we all look up from our texts to see what he's talking about. I have, he reads, 'Is an Arrow from the Almighty's Bow!' Oh, well, says Barb, but that's not part of it. How do you know? asks Fran. So, to shorten the narrative, we backed up steadily until we were in the prose address, 'To the Deists' on plate 52 of *Jerusalem*. There, after some trial and error, we discovered that there is a steady and calm beat to this prose, not at all the frantic or argumentative one the words seem to call for. And that beat is gently picked up and modulated by the quatrain which follows it. The rhythm gets more accent as the Quatrain moves into rhyming couplets which, then, swing easily into the 'first' line of Chapter 3 – and that tempo carries you wonderfully up to the line break of line 15. It happened before, you might say, our ears. And it was time to take a break. The faces of the people leaving the room were glowing. Franny's gift to us fell right in behind Jackie's. Now that we could all hear one another, all of us could see.

Remember: inspiration is only the first step, the taking in. What follows is the exhalation: the singing out. Blake says that "When this Verse was first dictated to me I consider'd a Monotonous Cadence like that used by Milton & Shakespeare & all the writers of English Blank Verse, derived from the modern bondage of Rhyming; to be a necessary and indispensable part of Verse. But I soon found that in the mouth of a true Orator such monotony was not only awkward but as much a bondage as rhyme itself. I therefore have produced a variety in every line, both of cadences & number of syllables."[56] What is varied, then, is not merely the number of syllables, but the tempo; not (as vocalization will show) the beat itself, but the swing. What I mean are the subtle shifts just before, on, and just after the beat which make what we call the "phrasing" of the singer. Blake is calling our attention here to the necessary retards and anticipation's which the moment and the emotion dictate in any vocal utterance. The word he employs is "cadences," and what it means is the control of the tempo that all performers use to mark their performances. What we love in the successful singer is as much his or her command of this blending of feeling and musicality as the strictly formal matters of pitch and resonance. It is what those passionate defenders of Callas refer to when their heroine is attacked for vocal excesses or coarseness. It is what we mean, in more common usage, by 'soul.' If you have it, even if the rest of your vocal apparatus is mediocre, you can hold the audience; if you don't have it, even if everything else is perfect, their minds (and souls) will wander. Tempo and cadence, of course, can only be *indicated* by the composer; they belong, ultimately, to the performer[57] and the moment. So they are realized precisely where Blake's language places them: "in the mouth of a true Orator." Readers, when they're using their tongues and ears, voices and bodies, are as much involved in the finishing of the work as an illuminator, using eyes and hands to realize a design. Both are informing the moment in the work. But simply scanning your eyes across the plate, silently turning the work into abstractions, you are no more than a computer; your eyes are reduced to seeing with, not through.

So. The next time I taught the Blake course, I took the next step. After all, hadn't the first thing Jackie suggested been that she might sing rather than carve a linoleum block? At the initial meeting with my new group of Jerusalem builders, I announced that in addition to carving and illuminating a linoleum block they were all going to sing. Details to follow. Sing? they said, You mean, like sing? I can't sing! You don't want to hear me sing! Wait. I said, One thing at a time.

In the next chapter I'll explain how the singing is managed. For now, consider this: if Blake is right – if everything is connected and there are no accidents – then Jackie and Fran are part, for me, of the meaning of Blake. As are each student who labored with me to perform his verses. As, now, you are as well.[58] And in these times when, owing to postmodern literary theories, the idea of a stable and permanent meaning[59] is under attack from all directions, can anyone object to the notion that Blake intends for us to come together, in a community, to discover what is waiting behind his traces in Eternity for us to assemble as Jerusalem? Consider too, that the dizzying complexity of his prophetic books is a perfectly reasonable strategy on Blake's part. For they constitute a deliberate and elaborate subversion of the idea of the (mass produced and uniform) book, itself a symbol of the mass produced and uniform society which worships it. Instead, each version of each plate of each version of each "book" is suited to the sung moment of its creation, in the individual being of its singer and his audience (like the *Popul Vuh*). And until I hear you singing, how can I know what we mean? If you can accept the idea that word plus design catalyzes an emergent and not entirely verbal meaning, why not take the next step with me? For I say that the word plus the voice brings us a living (what Blake called "Gothic") form, one which is communal and spontaneous and so escapes the stasis of what he called "mathematical" or "Grecian" form.[60] What Blake was trying to do – and what he succeeded at gloriously – was to prevent the completion of meaning because he understands that meaning, in our lives, is not perfected; it is performed. Singing Blake is not an elaboration or illustration of his meaning; it is the realization of it. We are winding into a ball, the golden string Blake has put into our hands.[61]

The Notion that man has a body Distinct From His Soul is to BE EXPUNGED

EMBrfEit

EMBrfEit.

Four: To Be Understood

Art bids us touch and taste and hear and see the world, and
shrink from what Blake calls mathematic form, from every
abstract thing, from all that is of the brain only, from all that
is not a fountain jetting from entire hopes, memories, and
sensations of the body.

W.B. YEATS, "The Thinking of the Body"[1]

We're seated in a circle; it's week four of the
Blake Course and tonight's meeting addresses *Songs of Innocence and
of Experience*. I look around at the faces: the whole group is present
tonight and, more importantly; they're all focused and alert. I am not
surprised, then, to hear myself saying: Right. Tonight we all sing. Find
a song you need or want to sing. Never mind if someone else chooses
the same one. I'll start and we'll just go round the circle. But no one
leaves until everyone has sung. Sit up; open up your ears – and throats.

We've already talked about spontaneous singing, how the melody
of the moment blends with the movement and weight of the words
to fill the air. It's what children do, easily and naturally – until they
learn to be embarrassed. But I'm not asking them now to talk about
it; I'm telling them to do it. Of course, they've been exchanging jour-
nal/notebooks for the past three weeks, and they've been learning
from one another's illuminations for the same period. They've been

discussing and experimenting with the Four Zoas in and out of class from the first assignments. So there is a high level of cohesion and trust in this group. Still, when I look up, they look stunned.

I'll go first, I say, and turn to my text. To my surprise, I choose "The Angel." There's no turning back, so I open my mouth and find a tune. It's not wonderful, but it isn't too bad. While I'm singing, I realize that increasingly, as the words in the verses point in one direction, the sound goes in the other. The result, oddly, is more sadness than confusion. I ask the class about this. A brief discussion ensues, tinged with unusual nervousness. In the silence that follows, I look to the person to my right. Marjorie? I ask. She gulps. We wait.

Then, in a halting voice that, line by line gets stronger and clearer, we hear the music of Blake's "Introduction" to *Songs of Innocence*. The fourth stanza is soft as kitten fur and we all share in her pleasure. The next person asks for a "pass." Sure, I say, we'll come back to you. The next person in the circle is Emily, a physics major. She looks like she's drowning.

You can't breathe, can you? I say. She nods her head, cheeks flaming. It's all right. Put your head down and take a breath; we'll get back to you. Next is Mari. She draws herself together – and sings "Ah! Sun-flower" in a voice so beautifully modulated that we listen like thirsty travelers from the desert finding water. Next to Mari is Kim. A ripple of nerves runs round the circle. Kim is the shyest person in the group. At the first meeting, after I introduced Fran Quinn to them as our resident expert on how to read poetry aloud, he made a point of engaging each member about his or her normal speaking voice. When he got to Kim, he had such difficulty getting her to talk, he assigned her to interrupt him at least once before the period was over. Tension mounted as the hour drew to its close and when she finally, hesitantly, almost painfully, broke in on him, we all cheered. And slowly, over the past weeks, she has been getting over her natural reticence.

Now all eyes are on her. She takes a deep breath – and stands up. We all shift uneasily. Is she going to leave the room? What will I do if she does? Slowly, deliberately, she turns her back to the circle. After a moment we hear her sweet voice weaving through "Infant Joy." When it falters, no one can tell whether the faltering is hers, or belongs to Blake's little song. She turns back around and sits down. Then, without lifting her eyes she says, It's not so bad. Really. Once you begin.

In that moment, I realize she's saved the day. We all know that no one could be shyer, or more afraid to sing in public, than Kim. So, no matter how scared any of us may be, we have no choice but to sing out. From that moment the fear and tension in the room dwindled from song to song. And when we come back to Emily, she sang, without hesitation, as easily and directly as a robin. It's not so bad. Really. Once you begin. So why does it *seem* so threatening?

You might try to explain it by saying we don't want to embarrass ourselves, because our voices are untrained, unskilled. Yet we easily, even joyfully, share our untrained and unskilled watercolor illuminations. For some reason "errors" of tint or line made by hand or eye seem far less threatening to us, far less embarrassing. I believe this is because the "illumination," seems more controlled and less revealing; it can even be separated from us. We can, after all, tear it up or conceal it; we can decide whether or not to acknowledge it as our own; we can proudly sign it, or "forget" to; we could even steal another's image and sign our own name to it. But we can neither separate ourselves from our voices, nor so easily control them; we can't "borrow" or trace another's voice, nor can we call back or cancel the sounds flowing from our mouths. We can only modulate and respond to them, exactly as – and in the moment with – our hearers. What we fear, then, is exactly the same thing we yearn for: the merger of ourselves with the source of our being. Children do this naturally, easily and unselfconsciously.[2]

When we speak our whole being – or sing it – we bring ourselves out of our own and into our hearers' hearts. Furthermore, we find in this moment that our hearers are not limited to our fellow humans, not even limited to the bodies around us in time and space. For, singing freely and openly, we discover what Blake did by the sea in Felpham, that late summer of 1800:

> My Eyes did Expand
> Into regions of air
> Away from all Care
> Into regions of fire
> Remote from Desire
> The Light of the Morning

Heavens Mountains adorning
In particles bright
The jewels of Light
Distinct shone & clear –
Amazd & in fear
I each particle gazed
Astonishd Amazed
For each was a Man
Human formd. Swift I ran
For they beckond to me
Remote by the Sea
Saying. Each grain of Sand
Every Stone on the Land
Each rock & each hill
Each fountain & rill
Each herb & each tree
Mountain hill Earth & Sea
Cloud Meteor & Star
Are Men Seen Afar[3]

Suddenly, we sense our continuity with the whole of creation. The experience is immediate and dynamic; not of an abstract, separable "meaning," but of a tangible, and connected knowing. The truth entering and leaving our bodies is shared, that is, not only intellectually, but physically and spiritually. So it's scary! Really scary. But it's not so bad. Really. Once you begin.

Physically, we are experiencing the *pneuma*, a fluid column of modulated air which rises from inside our chests and throats, then flows, in all directions, through that ocean of air on which our lives depend and through which we swim from birth to death. A portion of these rippling columns actually re-enters us, and is carried with infinite care to the inner ear where we, mysteriously, register it as sound. They also flow through and across our extremities; certain of these ripplings make our skin tingle, and our eyes fill up with tears. We recognize a great deal more in a person's voice than his thoughts; we register, as well, his emotion, his physical state and his spiritual one – in a word, the Four Zoas as constellated in him. Thus the *pneuma* may best be understood as the soul flowing through the moment and out into the cosmos – and back again.[4]

But the rational portions of our consciousness – our Selfhoods, or Egos – like to think of our speech as nothing more than a coded means of communication with other Egos, a simple turning of our thoughts into sounds. But, of course, spoken and sung words are incredibly rich and complex sounds – far richer and more complex than the abstract signs to which words are reduced in the dictionary. Emily's chest constricted so that she actually experienced difficulty, but not because she was having encoding difficulties. She was, rather, like Blake on the seashore: amazed and in fear.

What happens when we are fearful is that our lungs are prevented from filling by the constriction or "narrowing" of our chest; the word "anxious" is derived from the Latin "*augura*," "to narrow, or choke." But at the same time, our fearful body is demanding even more air – thus the drowning sensation. The reason fearful people "hold their breath" is that deep and full breathing intensifies and amplifies the fear – and all other feelings. So to avoid deepening their fear, they attempt to minimize it by controlling, constricting, their breathing. Most of us do the same thing whenever an unpleasant or uncomfortable feeling rises in us.

The problem is, of course, that that control minimizes pleasurable feelings as well as uncomfortable ones. And, trying to keep ourselves controlled and calm, we end by keeping ourselves rigid – and separated from our bodies as well as our feelings. But no amount of control can eliminate either the feelings – or the bodies having them. And since feeling and sensation are two of the Four Zoas, the more energy spent by the reasoning faculty suppressing them, the less energy available for truly rational dealing with the feelings. Help comes, – as it always must – not from the Ego, trapped in the self-perpetuating spiral, "becoming what [it] beholds,"[5] but from the generous one, Tharmas, whose quiet and simple gift soothes the fear and holds the key to balance: It's not so bad. Really. Once you begin, your body knows how to keep you moving. If it is Tharmas who moves you on a bicycle and a ski slope, so it is Tharmas, again, who brings you from your shaky beginning to real strength at the end of your song.[6]

Without this kind of personal, experiential knowing, Blake's fourfold vision seems little more than a quaint, abstract concept and his prophecies do, indeed, seem to be no more than a "plunge into wordy and boring unreality."[7] Hence, though it isn't necessary for us to "believe in" Christianity (Blake himself not only didn't "believe in" the church, he attacked it!),[8] it is essential that we explore the Four Zoas in ourselves. Fourfold vision, that is, is not a metaphor for the acquisition of Blake's philosophical or religious ideas; it is the means by which we apprehend his (and all true) art. The continuity of art and religion, truth and vision, is the foundation of Blake's work. If we return to Principles 5 & 7 of *ALL RELIGIONS are ONE*, Blake's introduction to the illuminated and prophetic works, we read:

> The Religions of all Nati-
> ons are derived from each
> Nations different reception
> of the Poetic Genius which
> is everywhere call'd the Spi
> rit of Prophecy.

> [and]

> As all men are alike
> (tho' infinitely vari-
> ous) So all Religions
> & as all similars have
> one source.
> The true Man is the
> source he being the
> Poetic Genius.[9]

The infinitely variable nature of the reception of truth and art is as important here as its unitary source. That is, in Blake's art we are not trying to achieve a unitary reading, a "supreme reality attained at last, the really real."[10] Instead, we are called to an individual voicing – and merging with – the Poetic Genius. Consider the design of the opening plate of *ALL RELIGIONS are ONE* [**Figure #2**].[11] What is immediately remarkable about it is its utter indifference to the requirements of both verisimilitude and fantasy. No child, viewing the strange scene[12] would imagine for an instant that the artist intends to represent either the natural wilderness – or a desert dream. It is an invitation – or a command. Look! it says, Open your eyes. Listen! Open your ears. Wake up! The voice crying in the wilderness is your own. Both hands point to the next page in your life as well as in the book.

Figure 2

In short, I believe the main barrier to the appreciation of Blake's work is opposition, not merely to the consideration, but even to the notice of the imaginative, rational, physical and emotive dynamic in the reception of art and the construction of meaning. And so, when we "read"[13] Blake, we sense immediately that something is missing. This is true when we have good facsimiles; something is still missing. And even when we hold a Blake original in our hands, we can sense a lack.[14] Isolated, a song is always a fragment, a piece removed from its larger context; melody is realized only in the hearer's heart. Acknowledging this lack is a beginning; lamenting it is all right, too – but we must do more: we must fill it in; inform it. And for that, we need one another.

The first time I meet with the students in my Blake course, after a brief description of what lies ahead, I talk with them for a moment about ringing. Every bell has its own tone, I say, no matter the shape and no matter the material, when its struck, it rings with its own, signature, tone. What about us? Do we not have our own voices? The vocal chords, whose pitch we change by constricting or relaxing them, hold the base signature tone we all have. When we're nervous, or anxious, the pitch rises because we "tighten up." And when we're relaxed and at ease, it drops to our own ringing. It's the relaxed tone that is our signature.

And then I ring for them. And I use a variation of the OM chant, starting with the open AH vowel, then shift to the OH sound by rounding my lips, and end with the UM sound by closing them. I look around then; almost all of them look a little uneasy; some are on the edge of giggling – and some are looking for an exit.[15] I use the notion of a signature tone to suggest to them what Fourfold vision might "look like." To begin with, I say, words mostly have a direct, literal meaning. As soon as you learn a language, you are able to say, My name is Jack. or The sky is red in the west. That is Single vision: the ratio is 1:1, the words say just what they say. But children, very early, make the great leap to Twofold vision. As soon as they realize that words can be applied wrong/rightly (that is, metaphorically), they do so – and they love it: You pig! they exclaim with delight as the language explodes all around them.

Many people never take the next step, from Twofold to Threefold vision. Maybe it's because the word "spiritual" comes to be associated in their minds with something weak, I don't know. But for others, there comes a time when the only words to say, and the right words, are: It's all right; it'll be all right. Yet both the sayer of those words and the hearer of them know that, for them, nothing will be all right, ever again. Still, there is something, beyond metaphor, beyond symbol, beyond language itself, that is truly addressed – and, somehow, really responds in the mystery of prayer. This is something like what Blake means by Beulah, the place of peace he associates with a Threefold vision.[16]

Notice that each time you move up, from Single to Twofold and from Twofold to Threefold vision, the size of the step expands exponentially. So how to explain the last leap – from Three to Fourfold vision? First, I say, remember that we're way beyond language now. And then I return to the ringing sound. Listen to me, I say, and I ring two or three times. Now, I say, you do it. Sit up and clear out your throats and RING! After a couple of practice runs, we get a stunning sound. When it dies out, I say, OK, now we're warmed up. I am going to start and then you're going to come in, when you feel it. And this time, nobody is going to lead; it's just going to happen exactly as it is supposed to happen and it will end exactly when it is supposed to end. There's no thinking here, no direction; just ringing. Each of us has two things to do: ring – as loud, as soft, and as long as you need to – and listen. Do both. When it is time to end, let it end.

I love the rich sound which follows. And I love, even more, what comes after. When the moment is right, I whisper: Did you hear it? The silence that comes after? That. [Silence.] Holds everything that is. Apprehension of the silence approximates, I think, what Blake means by Fourfold vision.

At subsequent class meetings, we open the session with similar vocalizing[17] so that we can bring our attention to one another and the present moment. When I sense that someone is wandering off (in their mind or body or feeling), and forgetting us, vocalizing is a good way to re-focus us all. In our busy, fractured world, most of us find it very hard to pay attention to the moment and one another. Some in the circle have never had anyone's undivided attention or given such attention to anyone – or anything – in their lives. But teaching (and learning) Blake is not something you do to or for someone; it is something you do with them and they with you. For, in the circle, whether you are speaking or silent, whether you are singing or listening, you are an equally vital and necessary part *of* it.

We have an example of such communal effort in Catherine Blake's finishing of her husband's illuminated works.[18] According to William Hayley, Blake's patron at Felpham, Catherine not only assisted him in his art, she drew, engraved, and sang with him and was, "…so truly the Half of her good Man, that they seem animated by one Soul."[19] Another early biographer, Allan Cunningham added that, "…she whom Blake emphatically called his 'beloved,' was no ordinary

woman. She wrought off in the press the impressions of his plates –
she coloured them with a light and neat hand – made drawings in the
spirit of her husband's compositions, and almost rivalled him in all
things save in the power which he possessed of seeing visions of almost any individual living or dead, whenever he chose to see them."[20]
Like Catherine, we may lack the power of seeing visions whenever we
choose, but we do not lack the power of seeing them at all.

W.B. Yeats, in a 1924 essay, "Literature and the Living Voice,"
writes that "most modern people [have forgotten] how to listen to serious words."[21] He recalled an earlier time – before men read silently,
and to themselves – when "the ear and the tongue were subtle, and
delighted one another with the little tunes that were in words; every
word would have its own tune." Then men loved their language and
literature was no more than, "*the perfection of an art that everybody prac-
tised.*"[22] But the inability of audiences to listen to serious words is only
part of the problem. There is also the inability to speak or sing them.
"Sometimes," he continues, "when some excellent man…has read me
a passage out of some poet, I have been set wondering what books of
poetry can mean to the greater number of men. If they are to read poetry at all, if they are to enjoy beautiful rhythm, if they are to get from
poetry anything but what it has in common with prose, they must hear
it spoken by men who have music in their voices and a learned understanding of its sound. There is no poem so great that a fine speaker
cannot make it greater or that a bad ear cannot make it nothing."[23]

Now Yeats is not simply mocking "poor readers;" he is calling our
attention to that tendency in the greater number of men to reduce the
experience of poetry – of art itself – to verbal analysis, what Blake
calls "Single vision." That a poem can be made greater by a good
reader, or made nothing by a bad ear, suggests the communal dynamic
of visionary art. Truth is emergent in it, flowing conjointly from the
work and from the audience. The badly read, or poorly heard, poem
is reduced to its "meaning," always something less than truth. But the
poem made greater, by either the voice of the reader or the ear of the
hearer restores truth in its communal harmony. When we are, as we so
aptly say, "moved" by a work of art, the movement is in our community as well as in ourselves. That is why all the faces around us are shin-
ing! And the movement is that of the Zoas in the direction of balance.

When they come to the eighth week, or mid-semester, the Blake seminar participants have illuminated, and shared, six of Blake's designs. They have sung to one another from the *Songs of Innocence and of Experience* and *The Book of Thel,* and they have composed and shared their own "Memorable Fancies." In addition to excerpts from Blake's letters and his Notebook, they have read and discussed all of the minor illuminated works. In the weeks of exchanging experiences in their journal/notebooks, they have become alert to the presence of the Four Zoas in their own lives as well. We are, by that time, a kind of family, speaking our own peculiar dialect and referring to a shared body of experience that is as emotional and sensational as it is intellectual and intuitive. So when I tell them that all we've done to this point is no more than preparation for the real work of the seminar; that from this point to the end of the semester our time will be taken up with *Milton* and *Jerusalem;* and that they will be doing the teaching, not me – they don't look stunned; they look eager.

I explain that I have broken up the two works into groups of plates to fit the time left – and the energies and faculties of the participants. Each member will work in two or three different groups (depending on the logistics of the seminar); and each group will be responsible to the entire seminar for the plates assigned to it. Each group, that is, must decide what they want to present to the seminar – and *how* to present it; there will be, as there always is, too much to do. As with the journal/notebooks, the illuminations, and the Memorable Fancy, there are – there can be – no rules for the presentation. But it must be a presentation, and must be addressed to *all the faculties;* thus, they may not simply lecture or report, any more than they may simply sing or paint. And they must, also, involve the entire seminar.

They are, in a word, *performing* their portions of *Milton* and *Jerusalem.* And they, as participants with the rest of us in Blake's vision, cannot attempt an abstract, or Platonic, presentation of a supposed objective "content" or "meaning." For they are seeking how best to present the emergent truth in these verses and designs, the truth for this community in this moment. What they are performing, that is, is dynamic and living; it cannot be recorded in this, or any, book, because it exists in the moment, in their experience – and their audience's – of presenting it.

Everyone participates and must be completely present – and ready to contribute when the moment requires it. I supply them all with Blake's advice to the artist, as it was remembered by his young disciple, Samuel Palmer:

> We must not begin with medium, but think always
> on excess, and only use medium to make excess more
> abundantly excessive.

> Genius is the unreserved devotion of the whole soul
> to the divine, poetic arts, and through them to God;
> deeming all else, even to our daily bread, only valu-
> able as it helps us to unveil the heavenly face of Beauty.

> Nature is not at all the standard of art, but art is the
> standard of nature. The visions of the soul, being per-
> fect, are the only true standards by which nature must
> be tried.[24]

When I go home that night, I know that the coming weeks will tell me whether or not the seeds I have planted have been supplied with enough nutrient. What I count on, and trust, is my memory of the first time it happened: coming home very late one night, because the time ran over and over and over, and waking my wife up to tell her: It's working! It's working. They're teaching me Blake!

But are they? Really? Maybe it's true that, as Blake says, "Jesus supposes every Thing to be Evident to the Child & to the Poor & Unlearned,"[25] but surely Blake didn't think that his own works were similarly transparent. And how can I imagine that my students will be able to find a way through the thickets of Blake's verse and designs and not get lost in wildernesses which have challenged the best efforts of the learned from his day to our own?

Take a breath. Close your eyes for a moment. Here is where you are. Now. So wait. Stop rushing on to the end of the sentence, think-ing that meaning will fall out of it like water from a tap. My belief that my students can teach Blake is based on my conviction that a com-munal understanding of him is the only one that can satisfy.[26] Truth is greater than meaning, and is a function of more than grammar and syntax, logic and number, all of which operate by division and analysis. And it is the existence of this dynamic, emergent truth that lies behind Blake's observation that, "when a Work has Unity it is as much in a Part as in the Whole."[27] Thus *Jerusalem* or *Milton*, having this unity, have it as much in the part as the whole. And this emergent meaning – or truth – can, indeed, be discovered even by beginners or students.

Take another breath. Listen *through*, the word, *through* the song – not *to* them. It is in this listening – and singing – that Blake finds a way back to Eden, to the restoration of the soul to unity. As he explains in the opening of The Four Zoas, "Los" is the name in this world (of time/space) of Urthona, the Zoa of intuition and inspiration in eternity. And the connection between these two worlds is "the Auricular Nerves of Human life / Which is the Earth of Eden."[28] "The Earth of Eden" – what can that mean? you ask. To answer you have to *listen*. For the music. Not for the notes or the words. But for the Music. Because music, too, is in the part as well as the whole. Otherwise, how can we know, as we do, immediately, the false note? The wrong reading? Even when it comes – as it did for Barb Bishop – at the beginning, making us stop and start over?[29]

Sing it, first, to yourself. Then sing it to those you know and trust. If we are to get from Blake anything more than the critic's explication, the teacher's notes, the doctrine of the theologian and/or priest, if we are to get the truth – we must HEAR it spoken, sung; it must ring through and break against our very bodies.[30] Everywhere in Blake's works we are called to sing and to hear.[31] For the end of his art is not the acquisition of power, but the realization of truth, which is heard in soul singing to soul, and building Jerusalem in harmony:

> Reader! lover of books! lover of heaven,
> And of that God from whom all books are given.
> Who in mysterious Sinais awful cave
> To Man the wond'rous art of writing gave,
> Again he speaks in thunder and in fire!
> Thunder of Thought, & flames of fierce desire:
> Even from the depths of Hell his voice I hear
> Within the unfathomd caverns of my Ear.

> Therefore I print; nor vain my types shall be:
> Heaven, Earth & Hell, henceforth shall live in harmony.[32]

Milton and *Jerusalem*, then, are prophetic texts, sung to communities by "Bards" like Ossian,[33] Daniel and Isaiah. Their significance or "meanings" cannot be realized strictly by the reasoning faculty or reduced to the understanding of the learned.[34] For they intend that rousing of the soul to action only supplied by the inspiration of the Poetic Genius in both singer and hearer. Blake asserts both the prophetic source of the Bard's Song in *Milton,* and truth's active purpose when the Immortals query the Bard:

> ...If it is true! if the acts have been perform'd
> Let the Bard himself witness. Where hadst thou this terrible
> Song
>
> The Bard replied. I am Inspired! I know it is Truth! for I Sing
> According to the Inspiration of the Poetic Genius
> Who is the eternal all-protecting Divine Humanity
> To whom be Glory & Power & Dominion Evermore Amen[35]

The meaning which the seminar members are sharing in their presentations or performances is not, then, something contained in words and music; it is something released by them. Truth is not so much a thing we know, as it is something we know again; something we recognize, just as we recognize ourselves and one another, in the sound of our voices. As Ferdinand Ebner, a modern theologian has put it:

> The interpretation of the Johannine Logos may be the last
> goal of that true philology which honors the secret of the
> Spirit and his revelation in the Word, something of which
> mere readers of the dead letter who are philologists for the
> sake of having a job, who have not been called by the Word
> and are incapable of becoming "hearers of the Word," naturally
> know nothing.[36]

One interprets the Logos, in Ebner's sense, by *hearing* it, by acting, participating in and with it. Thus Blake's personification of the Logos as the "The Holy Word, / That walk'd among the ancient trees" is perfectly consistent, since, in John's famous language, it is this Word by whom, "all things were [and are] made."[37] This Word, one of surpassing loveliness and unfailing strength, is and has always been a sung or *spoken* energy, not an abstract label. As the Psalmist puts it:

> Day unto day uttereth speech, and night unto night sheweth
>   knowledge.
> There is no speech nor language, where their voice is not
>   heard.
> Their line is gone out through all the earth, and their words to
>   the end of the world. In them he hath set a tabernacle
>   for the sun,
> Which is as a bridegroom coming out of his chamber…
>   …
>
> Let the words of my mouth, and the meditation of my heart,
>   be acceptable in thy sight, O Lord, my strength, and my
>   redeemer.[38]

Like David, Blake affirms the unity of Singer and song, and like him, he sees a unity of Creator and creature, in all things. For it is in the singing that we find ourselves one with our fellows, and in the sounding of our words we discover ourselves as we truly are: free of the mind-woven coverings that separate us from one another and leave us wandering in the night where, "the Starry Heavens are fled from the mighty limbs of Albion."[39] For, as Blake reminds us, the Fall of Man (into separation and selfhood), is not a temporal event as the Scribes have imagined, but an eternal one. The Incarnation, the Resurrection and the Last Judgment – none of these is understood by him to be singular events in time; instead he argues for their eternal reality; they inhere in each moment in time, insuring its lasting preservation:

> I am that Shadowy Prophet who Six Thousand Years ago
> Fell from my station in the Eternal bosom. Six Thousand
>   Years

> Are finishd. I return! both Time & Space obey my will.
> I in Six Thousand Years walk up and down: for not one
>   Moment
> Of Time is lost, nor one Event of Space unpermanent
> But all remain: every fabric of Six Thousand Years
> Remains permanent[40]

As it is we, ourselves, who have brought to ruin the Holy City, so it is we who must remain fallen – until we remember, with Albion, the surpassing loveliness of Jerusalem. For she eternally, "…walks upon our meadows green: / The Lamb of God walks by her side: / And every English child is seen, / Children of Jesus & his Bride."[41] It is, then, we who must rebuild the city. Here.

A work of art, like a performance, is a contract between artist and audience. A story begins, "A certain man planted a vineyard, and set an hedge about it…"[42] by immediately implying a connection between the teller and the hearers; it makes a promise to them. If the connection is broken and the promise not fulfilled, then the story is not a true one, the work of art fails.[43] When you are talking, that is, only to yourself, your hearers will detect it immediately – and stop listening. But when you believe in your audience, your audience senses your belief in them – and so they believe in you. This is the difference between argument and vision. The one asserts an abstract relation existing independent of its speaker and audience, the other reveals an eternal, shared and felt, truth.[44] Thus, says Blake, "When I tell any Truth it is not for the sake of Convincing those who do not know it but for the sake of defending those who Do."[45] Similarly, the seminar members, in presenting Blake's work, are defending or supporting those truth[s] which have emerged from their communal encounter; they are not trying to convince those who deny the necessity or importance of such community or encounter. Nor, if they are seriously speaking, is there any danger of our misunderstanding them. For as one of the greatest of the 'Proverbs of Hell' puts it: "Truth can never be told so as to be understood, and not be believ'd."[46]

The focus of this saying is on the *telling* of the truth. Knowledge, or the believing of truth depends on the perception of the speaker's good intention: when I tell the truth *so as to be understood,* then the hearer responds accordingly: by (actively) believing. For "knowledge," Blake writes, "is not by deduction but Immediate by Perception or Sense at once. Christ addresses himself to the Man not to his Reason."

The work of the seminar is to listen, in Yeats' language, to "serious words" spoken by men and women "who have music in their voices." More, they are speaking, and singing them "so as to be understood." An Eskimo poet, Orpingelik, of the Netsilik people, puts it in this way: "Songs are thoughts that are sung out with breathing when people let themselves be moved by a great force and no longer can be satisfied with ordinary speech."[47] That force which can no longer be satisfied with ordinary speech is also unable to contain itself in a single soul; it must spill out and be drunk up by the community which it informs.

While I'm writing these closing pages, I raise my eyes from the computer screen and see, just outside my window, a chickadee balanced on a wet black branch of my Japanese maple, bathing in and drinking gleaming rainwater from its red-black leaves. The whole scene is back-lit by brilliant sunlight so that the droplets flying from his feathers and from the leaves are like so many diamonds or falling stars. The truth inheres in things. We are connected. We feel this.

And so I was talking to Fran Quinn about how the presentations were going one day and I said, They're beautiful, you know, and fine. The kids are singing, and they're bringing in guitars and drums – and some are using watercolors and other visual supplements to their presentations. I just wish they weren't so stiff.

What do you mean, stiff? he asked.

Well, they get the rhythm in their voices, but their feet seem kind of glued to the floor.

Let's bring in Ann Igoe, he said.

Yeah. I said. I wish I'd thought of that.

Ann is a dancer and a teacher of dance. But she's much more. She has that fierce seriousness that goes with those whose art is full of joy. When you work with her, you work – but, and this is the important thing – you get moved. When you're finished with one of her sessions, you are not where you started, and you don't go back there, either. As Terri Banks wrote in her journal/notebook after our session with Ann: "Every inch of my body lives – and tonight I proved that!"[48]

Ann works by moving her dancers' attention to those blockages and hesitations which interfere with their natural grace and elegance. She begins by explaining that the universe *is* a dance; everything that is *is* *dancing*. If it were not so, it would all collapse in the blink of an eye. And then she begins moving – and moving you. It is infectious; you can't stand still or hold yourself back because she's there, beside you, before you can! With her attention on you like a spotlight, it's clear that it would be more embarrassing to freeze than it is to go with her. She makes you actually sense how crucial your movement is to the group; what a hole you would make in it were you to freeze or withdraw. So you pick it up. And so you experience, first hand, what W.B. Yeats meant when he sang, near the end of his life:

> God guard me from those thoughts men think
> In the mind alone;
> He that sings a lasting song
> Thinks in a marrow-bone[49]

Ann doesn't so much talk to or at you as take your hand, and push and pull your body, shifting you like you were so much sleeping clay. And then, suddenly, you have it – and she's gone like a breeze across the room. Melissa Krieger wrote that it was, "extremely free and personal. It was so intimate – trust and intimacy are walls that we all build around ourselves. Those walls get thicker as we grow older – or so it seemed before. But I guess certain people just know how to break through or climb over. I couldn't believe how comfortable I felt. Now I feel everything and I guess maybe that scares me. Anyway, I felt a part of myself pried open in the dancing. It's a part that I hope never to close again."[50]

But Ann works for more than individual opening or dancing. When she judged that we were ready, she took us, in groups of four or five, which she placed in complex and interlocked positions. As the rest of the seminar made a ring round those so placed, Ann had them close their eyes and wait for the music to tell them when and how to move; then they were to dance, together, with their eyes closed so that they could focus on sound and rhythm – and touch. We in the audience held our breath. There was a silence, then the music came up – and we were amazed to see the spontaneous flowering of a communal beauty out of those people whom we had seen before only as individuals. Their bodies moved like the pieces of glass in a kaleidoscope, making one beautiful and striking pattern after another. And they came to a natural conclusion with the music in the same way that our spontaneous chanting comes to that compelling silence. Susan Rudolph spoke for all of us when she wrote: "I live my life through my eyes, which are everything to me, yet it seemed when I closed them, when I danced with my eyes closed, I saw more of me. I didn't have to know who was watching me; maybe I didn't want to. I want to say: Don't talk to me about what you saw; I heard it already in your unseen stare: Life is lovely to look at, you are beautiful to look at – in anger, in pain – someone is always watching. Someone is always exposing themselves to you, unspoken. Someone wants to caress the deepest part of you, of life, that someone might be me."[51]

As is always the case, I only see in Blake what is there after I have been taken by the hand by someone like Jackie, my blind singer, or Franny or Ann or my wife or one of my teachers – all those who have studied and loved Blake with me; all those who have trusted me and given me their trust in return; all those who have worked with me in my life. And so, after dancing with Ann, I picked up my Blake and read again, for the first time, his prayer for us all:

> In my Exchanges every Land
> Shall walk, & mine in every Land,
> Mutual shall build Jerusalem:
> Both heart in heart & hand in hand.

This everlasting building implies a constant searching for form, a continual emergence of truth and the everlasting renewal of art. And it is in this open space, this incompletion, that my seminar has been permitted to exist. Louise Glück, in a beautiful essay directly addresses this phenomenon, of all true, that is, religious, art. "I do not think," she writes, "that more information always makes a richer poem. I am attracted to ellipsis, to the unsaid, to suggestion, to eloquent, deliberate silence. The unsaid, for me, exerts great power…Such works inevitably allude to larger contexts; they haunt because they are not whole, though wholeness is implied: another time, a world in which they were whole, or were to have been whole, is implied."[52] It is this which we feel in Blake; this is the "golden string" he hands us. And it will take us, indeed, to Heaven's Gate, where we must, together, dance and sing Jerusalem into being again.

Each of us must attend to what is actually present: the poem, song, or design awaits our active, that is, formal completion of it. For everything must have a form – and it's by their forms that we know [all] things [that we, really, *know*].[53] It is a minutely particular form and calls out to the minutely particular in our own being for its completion. There is, Blake says, "neither character nor expression without firm and determinate outline…. The great and golden rule of art, as well as of life, is this: That the more distinct, sharp, and wiry the bounding line, the more perfect the work of art."[54]

This sharp, distinctive form is a harmonious and proportionate identity beckoning, in its clarity, to our own unique physical, emotional, spiritual and intellectual identities. In its minutely particular and eternal form, Blake's work directs us, not to the alikeness of things, but to their wonderful, myriad, particular voices and faces, voices we must work to hear, faces we must work to see.[55] For all of us – while we are here in this place and at this time – are here to work toward knowing.[56]

Postlude: A Memorable Fancy

Let every Christian as much as in him lies engage himself openly & publicly before all the World in some
Mental pursuit for the Building up of Jerusalem

WILLIAM BLAKE, *Jerusalem* 77

Music serves a grand function in this crazy old world,
and all of us, one way or another, are singers. Let your
song fly. The rest of us need it.

KELLY JOE PHELPS, *Roll Away the Stone*[1]

I was talking, one afternoon, to Tom Devine. He had graciously read my manuscript and supplied me with thoughtful notes. He said, You know your book offers a solution to one of the more nagging problems with *Jerusalem*. What's that? I asked. Well, as everyone knows, the fourth Chapter arrives at the stunning vision of the identification of all things in the Eternal Humanity Divine and the embrace of Albion and Jerusalem at last which is the subject of the beautiful illumination below the final words. But that, though it is clearly labelled, THE END OF THE SONG OF JERUSALEM it is not the end of the book. There's one more page, the final plate, Number 100.

Yes, I said, I guess it always seemed to me that he had juggled his full plate illuminations and introductory matter to make the thing come out with a round hundred plates. And it does make the last plate a little anti-climactic.

But your book, said Tom, makes it clear why that has to be the case, doesn't it? Because when you complete the poem you have to turn the page and return to this place, where you discover the unending task which is the subject of that last plate: "Los, with his tools, happily building Jerusalem. So the title of your book is perfect: Blake knew, and told us clearly, that the work is always just beginning with him; never ending.

So I thanked Tom then, and thank him publically, now. I didn't know when it was given to me what my title meant. Or what it could mean. But that's been my experience with Blake, and my life, since I began. And so, in the spirit of this book, I don't end with me or with Blake, but with the labors of Los. Here let me share with you a Memorable Fancy as it was delivered to me by one of the builders of Jerusalem, Alisa Pykett:

A memorable fancy

Alison Pykett

I ran on the paved path until the sky skyscrapers vanished and the noise faded. I began to walk when I reached the valley between the mountains. I came up to a lake and I stared at my reflection; gradually I could see the image of a native man wearing only a loin cloth. I asked him where he came from and he replied, "I have traveled with you all this time but this is the first moment that you really looked at anything. You looked deep into the water and saw first yourself and then me." "Who the hell are you?" I asked as I noticed the peaceful, relaxed look of his body he answered, "yes, hell does have a lot to do with who I am, but so does heaven.

You see, I exist within the [3] contraries. I am Blake" The more I watched him, the more solid he seemed, but even with his solid form, he was weightless in the air. It supported him.

He continued, "I am glad you[4] have finally decided to leave your lopsided existence on the highway but now you must search out what your new existence will be. Your old view was warped, do you realize this now? You sat at your desk and allowed Urizen to rule your life, while you hid your old clients, Luvah, Tharmas, and Urthona in the back supply room. You ignored their cries as you went back to grab more staples. You overwhelmed yourself with reason and your life made sense, in the conditions of the paperwork

Why is it that you had to flee [6]
from the paved world
at a dead sprint?"

"Now stop. **LOOK** at where you "
are. What do you feel? What
do you hear? No, don't look
with your eyes! Look, hear, feel
and touch with your entire
body. Have you ever listened
through your legs and felt
the vibration of sound pulsing
through your muscles and you
blood? Open up all the senses
in your body and feel parts of you
come alive that you have tried
to box up for years.

Do you see that mountain? Go
and embrace it."
I started to walk towards the
mountain, trying to figure out
what to do. How do I embrace
a mountain that is hundreds
of times my size? He could
tell by the expression on my
face that I was thinking too
much. He yells, "Too much
'Irizen'! Just embrace the
Mountain!"

As he glanced at my puzzled face, still displaying the efforts of Urizen, he called me back. He started explaining to me again; "My people use the Medicine Wheel as a symbol for balance that they need to maintain in their lives. I always try to stay in the middle of this wheel with my four different Zoas. The Medicine Wheel can apply to any aspect of my life that I wish — the directions, colors, or my total being. Urthona comes in from the North like the sea guiding with its waves. Urizen stands in the South like the rocks

that hold the sea from flooding
the earth. Tharmas is in
the West like the tree that
feels the wind and the rain against
its rough bark. Luvah resides
in the East like the fruit that
the tree bears. This Medicine
Wheel continually moves, but it
always has balance. It does
not balance me directly, though,
because I am only a small part of
the world. The Wheel balances
the whole world, and, since I live
in this world, I absorb the
balance of it through all four of my Zoas."

I thought about what Blake"
had told me and I headed towards
the mountain. I climbed and
climbed all the way up to the
top and then I jumped off,
expecting to find balance in
my free flight through the air.
All I found was a painful collision
with the earth when I landed.
I thought that I had understood
Blake, so now I was more
bewildered than before.

"My fellow human," he said. "I told you to pay attention to the world and yourself, right? So why would you ignore your body, your physical self, and try to make it act in a way for which it is not properly created. You are not a bird; you have no wings to fly.

Listen to your body and be ¹³
aware of what it can do. The
earth holds the energy. It also
lives in balance with the
medicine wheel; it gives us life.
Why would you search for balance
away from it? Ground yourself
in the energy of the earth and
then you will be closer to your
natural balance."

I reflected for a moment and [14]
began listening to my body. I know
Tharmas needed touch, Luvah
needed someone to hold her. Urthona
needed to be set free, and Urizen
needed peace. I again walked
towards the mountain and I
approached the incline. I laid down
on the ground and I felt the
earth rhythm pulsing through
my blood. My mind was calm
and I felt like I could let my
body fall into the earth's embrace.
Urthona smiled. Urizen gave an
exhausted sigh of relief.
        I was home.

I turned onto my back[15]
and I looked back at Blake.
He Sang:

Welcome to the world,
my newborn babe!

Notes

PRELUDE: A GOLDEN STRING

1. *Milton,* 2:25 [Erdman, 96]. Unless otherwise specified, all citations from Blake are taken from the Erdman's standard edition: *The Complete Poetry & Prose of William Blake* (Newly Revised Edition), ed. David V. Erdman; Commentary by Harold Bloom: (Anchor Books, New York, 1988).

2. "The Mental Traveller" [Erdman, 485].

3. Henry Crabb Robinson in Bentley, *Blake Records,* 313.

4. *Milton* 29:4-9 [Erdman, 127] A cubit being the distance from the elbow to the tip of the forefinger (18-22 inches), he means an elevation around 40 feet, a fair measure for the rooftop of a single story dwelling. The universe visible from such a vantage is one in which there are more than sufficient opportunities for corporeal acts of charity and love.

5. "Little Girl Lost," *Songs of Innocence* [Erdman, 20] See epigraph to Prelude, p.1.

6. Quoted by Bentley in *Blake Records,* 302.

7. Experienced Blakeans will recognize here the Four Zoas (Tharmas, Urizen, Luvah & Los); beginners are encouraged to forget about their names until they have located their functions and energies *first hand* in themselves. Their energy and conflict is present right now inside you as you read this. It is chaotic and noisy, but it's there. At this point it is only necessary that you remember "Four Mighty Ones are in every Man" (*Four Zoas* 1 [Erdman, 300]). How these Mighty Ones are (mysteriously) unified is suggested by Blake's enumerating the following verses from *John* on his poem's title page:

> That they all may be one; as thou, Father, art in me, and I in thee, that they also may be one in us: that the world may believe that thou hast sent me.

And the glory which thou gavest me I have given them; that
they may be one, even as we are one:
I in them, and thou in me, that they may be made perfect in
one; and that the world may know that thou hast sent me,
and hast loved them, as thou hast loved me. (17:21-23),

and:

And the Word was made flesh, and dwelt amongst us, (and we
beheld his glory, the glory as of the only begotten of the
Father,) full of grace and truth. (1.14) *King James Version*

8. Notebook, N54 [Erdman, 520]. In another place, Blake identifies the windows as "Four Caverns rooting downwards their foundations," (*Four Zoas* 6:263 [Erdman, 351]) highlighting both their organic
natures and their divine origin and purpose: they root downwards into
time/space in order to connect us to Eternity/Infinity. (The familiar
five senses are reduced by Blake to four by combining touch and taste.
See *Milton* 5:19-37 [Erdman, 99].) This suggestive mingling of Nordic
and Judaeo-Christian myth is probably deliberate on Blake's part; his
is a continuing effort to escape from petrified or orthodox readings of
reality.

9. "I must Create a System, or be enslav'd by another Mans /
I will not Reason & Compare: my business is to Create" (*Jerusalem*
10:20 [Erdman,153]). The point, that is, is not that systems are bad,
but that anyone careful enough to create a system, *and understand that
he is creating it,* is far less likely to be enslaved by it. One of Los's (that
is the Imagination's intuitive energy in man), tasks is "Striving with
Systems to deliver Individuals from those Systems" (*Jerusalem* 11:5,
[Erdman,154]).

10. "He who sees the Infinite in all things sees God. He who sees
the Ratio only sees himself only." (*No Natural Religion*, [Erdman, 3]).

11. *The Laocoön*, [Erdman, 274].

12. *The Marriage of Heaven and Hell*, 21 [Erdman, 42].

13. *Jerusalem* 77 [Erdman, 231].

14. Letter 23, to Thomas Butts, 22 Nov. 1802 [Erdman, 722].

15. W.J.T. Mitchell, *Blake's Composite Art*, xv.

16. James Bogan & Fred Goss eds.; North Atlantic Books: Richmond, CA. 1982.

17. —— 127-140.

18. "Annot. Siris," [Erdman, 663].

19. "The Everlasting Gospel," e14, [Erdman, 524].

ONE: BEGINNING WITH BLAKE

1. Luke 24:13-51 *King James Version.* My reading in light of my understanding of the nature of Blakean reality is, of course, not informed by standard principles of Biblical exegesis, either of Blake's time or my own. All such treatments, or readings of textual materials are alike in their assumption that words are abstract symbols rather than movements of air in real time from a living throat, that is spiritual exhalations. The difference is similar to that between the Hebrew, 'dabhar' and the Greek, 'Logos.' The former, as I understand it, refers to a constitutive energy, antecedent to the reality it speaks or "calls" into being. But the word, in Greek, is the reverse, it assumes the prior existence of the thing named. For the Greeks, that is, – and for most of us still under their influence, words are merely secondary and abstract symbols, not primary and catalytic agents. Blake, needless to say, favors the Hebrew sense over the Greek.

2. *Urizen* 2:8.39-40 (Plate 4), [Erdman, 72].

3. Quoted in Bentley, *Blake Records*, 310-11.

4. Blake's Notebook, 21, [Erdman, 501].

5. And see "Auguries of Innocence": "He who Doubts from what he sees / Will neer Believe do what you Please / If the Sun & Moon should Doubt / Theyd immediately Go out" [Erdman, 492].

6. See the Annotations to Watson's *Apology for the Bible,* [Erdman 611]; Thornton's *The Lord's Prayer, Newly Translated,* [Erdman, 667]; and *The Works of Joshua Reynolds,* [Erdman 635]. Remember, too, that "...the vioice of honest indignation is the voice of God." (*The Marriage of Heaven and Hell,* pl. 12; [Erdman, 38]). I can't help noticing that Erdman's copy editor missed the error in spelling the word *voice* here; and since there are, indeed, no mistakes, it is wonderful that they choked on the word *voice.*

7. *Milton* 40 [46]:12-41; [48]:28; [Erdman, 141-2], PUNCTUATION ADDED for clarity.

8. Quoted by Alan Riding in *The New York Times,* Sunday, June 28, 1998, Section 2, 10.

9. Blake is a Christian poet and efforts to study him apart from his Christianity are about as sensible as studying Dante, or Rumi, or the Psalmist apart from their religious contexts. On the other hand, what Blake *means* by "Christianity" is at odds with all known – or imaginable! – credos, branches and/or denominations. His definition of the Christian is as simple as it is demanding: "A Poet a Painter a Musician an Architect: The Man / Or Woman who is not one of these is not a Christian / You must leave Fathers & Mothers & Houses & Lands if they stand in the way of ART" *The Laocoön,* [Erdman 274].

10. *Milton* 21[23]:12-14, [Erdman, 115].

11. *Milton* 5:28-33, [Erdman, 99] PUNCTUATION ADDED for clarity. In his brilliant book, *What Painting Is,* James Elkins elucidates how the artist senses this interpenetration: "An artist has a delicate sense of the work to come and how it might become the perfect thing in the imagination, but historians and critics are wrong to assume that it can be clearly seen in advance. No painter knows what the picture will look like, and those painters who try too hard to use paint to realize an idea are typically disappointed. Like poetry or any other creative enterprise, painting is something that is worked out in the making, and the work and its maker exchange ideas and change one another." It seems unnecessary to point out that life, if it is anything, must be a creative enterprise. Efforts to make it conform to our ideas of it in advance certainly lead to disappointment! That the work and the worker interpenetrate will be a feature of my argument as well. *What Painting Is: How to Think About Oil Painting, Using the Language of Alchemy,* London and New York; Routledge, 1999, 78.

12. Even Newton has to face the problem of how objects supposedly separated from one another are nonetheless observed to influence one another at a distance. He famously measured and reduced this mysterious relationship to formula. Gravity still is, for all our measurement of it, little more than a word for something we must take on faith but cannot understand.

13. *Jerusalem* 25:7-8, [Erdman 170] And see also: "A Robin Red breast in a Cage / Puts all Heaven in a Rage" "Auguries of Innocence," 5-6, [Erdman, 490].

14. "The Chinese Written Character as a Medium for Poetry" ed. John Kasper, "Square Dollar Series," New York, n.d. quoted by Donald Davie in *Articulate Energy: An Inquiry into the Syntax of English Poetry*, London: Routledge & Kegan Paul, 1976, 35.

15. *The Four Zoas* 1 (17) 2-7, [Erdman, 310].

16. "…the Philosophy of Causes & Consequences misled Lavater as it has all his contemporaries. Each thing is its own cause & its own effect   Accident is the omission of act in self & the hindering of act in another, This is Vice but all Act [<*from Individual propensity*>] is Virtue. To hinder another is not an act it is the contrary it is a restraint on action both in ourselves & in the person hindered. for he who hinders another omits his own duty. at the time // Murder is hindering Another / Theft is hindering another / Backbiting. Undermining C[i]rcumventing & whatever is Negative is Vice / But the or[i]gin of this mistake in Lavater & his contemporaries, is, They suppose that Womans Love is Sin. in consequence all the Loves & Graces with them are Sin" Annotat. Lavater, 88 [Erdman, 601].

17. *Milton* 26:44-45, [Erdman, 124]. See also his response to Bacon's comment that "while the mind of man looketh upon second (i.e.. 'natural') causes scattered, it may sometimes rest in them and go no farther." To this Blake replies: "There is No Such Thing as a Second Cause nor as a Natural Cause for any Thing in any Way   He who says there are Second Causes has already denied a First The Word Cause is a foolish Word" "Annot. Bacon," 76-7, [Erdman, 626]. And see: "We who dwell on Earth can do nothing of ourselves, every thing is conducted by Spirits, no less than Digestion or Sleep. [*to Note the last words of Jesus: All power is given unto me in heaven and in earth*]" *Jerusalem* 3, [Erdman 145] The words from Matthew (28:18) are etched by Blake in Greek characters.

18. Annot Lavater: 630, [Erdman, 599] PUNCTUATION ADDED for clarity.

19. I shouldn't have to, but I find that many of my students, as a consequence of decisions made by their spiritual educators, are unfamiliar with the words of Jesus, including these beautiful ones: "Are not two sparrows sold for a farthing? and one of them shall not fall on the ground without your Father" (Matt 10:29).

20. I especially like the observation by one of Peter Matthiessen's American Indian characters: "You will say all of this is funny coincidence, but if you was Indin, you would understand it. Indins don't know about coincidence, that is just white-man talk." Blake would, I think, agree. See *Killing Mr. Watson*, New York: Random House, Vintage Books, 1991, 104.

21. *Marguerite Yourcenar, With Open Eyes: Conversations with Matthieu Galey*, (trans. Arthur Goldhammer) Boston: Beacon Press, 1984, 185-6.

22. See I Corin. 1:10 & 14:40.

23. Numbers 11:29 And see *Milton* 1, [Erdman, 96].

24. *Four Zoas*, marginal lines following 1:329, [Erdman, 825].

25. I've asked students and colleagues repeatedly about their favorite class notebooks. Invariably they confess, with some shyness, that the only ones they've kept, the only ones they think are worthwhile, are full of doodles and strange drafts of things – letters, poems, songs, dreams, sketches – which somehow got started by something that was said or happening in the class, but which had "nothing to do" with the lecture or class. Why is this no surprise?

26. *The Marriage of Heaven and Hell* 4, [Erdman, 34]. PUNCTUATION ADDED for clarity.

27. "Annot Lavater" 630, [Erdman, 599] And see Prelude notes 2 & 6.

28. Ephesians 6:12 (King James Version) Blake quotes these words in Greek on the title page of *The Four Zoas*, [Erdman, 300].

29. F.R. Leavis, "Justifying One's Valuation of Blake," a lecture given at Bristol University, 15 November, 1971 and reprinted in *William Blake: Essays in Honor of Sir Geoffrey Keynes* (Oxford: Clarendon Press, 1973), 67. It must be assumed that Blake and Leavis are, in Eternity, the best of friends since Leavis has been true to himself and forthrightly stated what many lesser folk have thought but feared to say. For, as Blake wrote in a letter to Butts, "the Man may be the friend of my Spiritual Life while he seems the Enemy of my Corporeal but not Vice Versa." (Letter 26, April 25, 1803; [Erdman, 728]).

30. *Milton* 2:25; 3:5; 4:20; 7:18; 50; 9:7; 11:31 [Erdman, 96-105].

31. "A Note on the Texts," M.L. Johnson & J.E. Grant, eds. in *Blake's Poetry and Designs* (A Norton Critical Edition) New York and

London: W.W. Norton, 1979, xliii.

32. Preface to *Milton,* [Erdman, 95].

33. "Annot. to Reynolds," xlvii [Erdman, 639].

34. *A Vision of The Last Judgment,* [Erdman, 563]. PUNCTUATION ADDED for clarity.

35. *Jerusalem* 32 [36]:51-56, [Erdman, 179]. That what only *seems* to us to be can become our reality is a proof of the constitutive power of the word and our imagination and is a theme repeated in Blake's prophetic books in which we often find agents 'becoming what they behold.' See, for instance, *Four Zoas* 4:201-4; [Erdman, 336]; *Milton* 3:29, [Erdman, 97] and *Jerusalem* 30 [34]:54, [Erdman, 177].

36. Letter 88 to G. Cumberland, 12 April, 1827, [Erdman, 783]. PUNCTUATION ADDED for clarity.

37. *Jerusalem* 55:56-63, [Erdman, 205].

38. *Descript. Catalogue,* [Erdman, 543] And see also *ALL RELIGIONS are ONE,* Principle 6, [Erdman, 1].

39. My response to the charge that such evidence is anecdotal would be the one my wife (a therapist) gave to a statistical reasoner at a party: "All real evidence is anecdotal."

40. *ALL RELIGIONS are ONE,* Principle 1, [Erdman, 1] and *Milton* 2:8, [Erdman, 96].

41. *A Vision of The Last Judgment* [Erdman, 565-6].

42. "Several Questions Answerd" [Erdman, 474-5].

43. See Erdman, 789 and *The Early Illuminated Books,* eds. Eaves, Essick & Viscomi (The William Blake Trust) Princeton Univ. Press, Princeton, N.J. 1993, 9-41.

44. "The caption quotes all four Gospels (Matthew 3.3, Mark 1.3, Luke 3.4, John 1.23) and indicate that the figure is John the Baptist preaching in a wilderness represented by foliage and tree trunks… thus Blake implies that he sees himself as continuing in the tradition of John the Baptist, just as John repeats the message of Isaiah 40.3." Eaves, Essick & Viscomi, *Early Illuminated Books,* 34. The plate is reproduced as Figure #2 [97].

45. *ALL RELIGIONS are ONE,* Eaves, Essick, Viscomi, 46-7; [Erdman, 1].

46. *THERE is NO NATURAL RELIGION* [Erdman, 2-3].

47. I know (and Blake knew) that there is an "historical context" to our lives. He also knew that the notion of an objective or "historical reading" of events and persons is, like all abstractions, a dream and delusion of Ulro. See *Four Zoas* 7:331, (85, 1.21) [Erdman, 360] and *Milton* 29 [31]:15-17, [Erdman,127]. See also Blake's remark: "I am really sorry to see my Countrymen trouble themselves about Politics. If Men were Wise the Most arbitrary Princes could not hurt them If they are not Wise the Freest Government is compell'd to be a Tyranny." "Public Address," [Erdman, 580].

48. See Matt. 22.2-14.

49. *VISIONS of the Daughters of Albion,* motto [Erdman, 45].

50. *The Marriage of Heaven and Hell,* 5, [Erdman, 34].

51. Matthew 22:1-14.

52. "Annot. Watson" [Erdman, 617].

53. *Descriptive Catalogue,* [Erdman, 544].

54. Letter To Trusler 23 Aug 1799 [Erdman, 702].

55. "Annot. Berkeley's Siris," [Erdman, 664].

56. Ibid.

57. Letter to Dr. Trusler, 23 August, 1799 [Erdman, 702].

58. One of my readers, Ann Igoe, taking my words to heart about challenging teachers, wrote on an early manuscript at this point: "What about Blake's isolation? Wasn't he totally alienated from his culture?" No. In fact, he always had Mrs. Blake – and though the scholars don't like this arrangement, the evidence we have points to a considerable involvement in his work. In addition, though he quarreled with them, Blake had a number of friends and patrons. Finally, in his later years, he had a group of disciples, young painters and poets. Indeed, there may well be an interesting connection to be found between Blake's periods of original production and the size and quality of his community of friends.

59. See Harold Bloom's note on the Title of *The Four Zoas.* [Erdman, 948].

60. Experienced readers of Blake will be aware that my descriptions are sketchy and no substitute for repeated immersion in Blake's work. For instance, the naming of the Zoas is much more complex than these four suggest, for each of them has more than one name, as well as what Blake labels an "Emanation." I am, however, less attempting to catalog what is essentially fluid, than I am trying to orient beginners to these energies in themselves and in their companions in the task of building Jerusalem.

61. Tharmas' name begins with the English "thorn" [þ] or "th" sound made by placing the tip of the tongue just under the upper front teeth and blowing air past it; the first vowel "ah" is immediately shaped by the "r" that follows it, making the tongue drop and curl while the lips form an "o" shape which then are shut to make the "m." Finally, the "ah" vowel comes back and the tongue jumps back and up to the palate to make the hissing "s" at the end. "Tharmas," the word, dances in our mouth the way our bodies dance in the world. "Urthona," like Urizen, sounds like an English phrase, in this case "Earth Owner." None of this speculation is as important as noting that Blake refuses to employ the terms already in existence to categorize experience. Urizen, that is, is NOT only reason. And not only Your reason. Reason, in fact, is a pale suggestion, a limited and defined category of thought for an energy which, in reality, goes beyond thought's capacity. The same goes for all the Zoas!

62. *Milton* 1, [Erdman, 95-6] The Zoas in ( )'s are my suggestion, not Blake's.

TWO: IN THE PALM OF YOUR HAND

1. Jackie Miller, submitted Jan 21, 1992. Used by permission. Jackie's reading is, of course, her reading, not *the* reading. It's her courage and confidence that were infectious. Blake asks and expects no more and no less.

2. Nelson Hilton, *Literal Imagination: Blake's Vision of Words* Berkeley, Los Angeles & London: University of California Press, 1983, 1.

3. Though Blake only used the term "illuminated printing" in a "Prospectus" he etched, according to Gilchrist, in 1793 (*Life of Blake,* 1863, II, 263-4), Blake scholars have generally employed it to indicate the peculiar relationship between Blake's designs and his texts, one that would be confused by using the term "illustrations." When he supplied coloring and added (or deleted) details to the printed plates, the term Blake ordinarily used for the process was, "finishing." See, for example the letters of Blake to Hayley (25 April 1805) [Erdman, 763] and Linnell (Feb 1827) [Erdman, 782]. Since what I am asking the students to do is very much the same thing, it seems fair to call their work "Illuminations" – always keeping in mind Blake's admonition that, "No Man Can Improve An Original Invention." *Public Address,* [Notebook, 62], Erdman, 576.

4. It is the "Hirelings" in Camp, Court and University, who, by their preoccupation with "universal truth" and suppression of individual vision, "depress Mental & Prolong Corporeal War." The process is described by Ololon in the poem at 34 [38]: 49- 35 [39]:6, Erdman, 134-5.

5. "What are all the Gifts of the Spirit but Mental Gifts[?;] whenever any Individual Rejects Error & Embraces Truth a Last Judgment passes upon that Individual" *A Vision of The Last Judgment* [84], Erdman, 562.

6. *Milton,* 1: Preface, Erdman, 96.

7. —— 95.

8. "Annot. Watson" [15], Erdman, 617.

9. It should be clear to attentive readers that, for the most part, this was the story of my academic career. The great teachers I had, beginning with Dr. Carl Enoch William Dahlstrom, unfailingly left me with an awareness of their sadness at my refusal to contend vigorously enough with them and their ideas. Good teachers all, though, they also hoped, one day, to see me wake from the sleep they only disturbed a little.

10. "What is that Talent which it is a curse to hide? What are the Treasures of Heaven which we are to lay up for ourselves, are they any other than Mental Studies & Performances?" "To the Christians" *Jerusalem* 77, Erdman, 231.

11. *The Marriage Heaven and Hell,* 12, 153.

12. This diagram is described in *Milton* 34 [38]:32-37 and is reproduced in Erdman's edition on p. 133.

13. There are several accounts of the Zoas' fall from unity or balance; Luvah is said to have assumed Urizen's sphere; see *Milton* 19:15-26, Erdman, 112-13; *Milton* 34[38]: 38-9; *Jerusalem* 32:31-37, Erdman 178; *Jerusalem* 46[32]:7, Erdman 195; *Jerusalem* 74:4-9, Erdman 229; *Jerusalem* 98:12-23, Erdman 257. Urizen, too, often speaks as though he had usurped Urthona's sphere. The imbalance, of course, must have as many manifestations as there are wobbles in the gyroscope winding down.

14. As the course goes forward, in fact, students bring their work earlier and earlier to the classroom in order to have more time to examine and talk about each other's work.

15. *A Vision of The Last Judgment,* Erdman, 554 [Punctuation mine. By supplying no punctuation in the last sentence, he creates a delightful ambiguity, which is lost whether a single comma is placed after "pray", or, as I have done, it is set off with two commas].

16. Henry Crabb Robinson, in Bentley, *Blake Records,* 311.

17. "Jesus supposes every Thing to be Evident to the Child & to the Poor & Unlearned Such is the Gospel The Whole Bible is filled with Imaginations & Visions from End to End & not with Moral Virtues that is the baseness of Plato & the Greeks & all Warriors The Moral Virtues are continual Accusers of Sin & promote Eternal Wars & Domineering over others" "Annot. Berkeley's *Siris,*" 215, Erdman, 664.

18. "He who would do good to another, must do it in Minute Particulars / General Good is the plea of the scoundrel hypocrite & flatterer" *Jerusalem* 55: 60-1, Erdman, 205.

19. In this context, the Notebook poem, "What is it men in women do require," (Erdman, 474) makes perfect sense. It is not our own satisfaction we require of others, but *their* satisfaction (which comes with self-realization).

20. *THERE is NO NATURAL RELIGION* [b] V & VII Erdman, 2-3.

21. Who, in these litigious times, can be unaware that law, (a mill with complicated wheels) far from protecting goodness and punishing evil, only reward legality, and that only to the highest bidder?

22. *THERE is NO NATURAL RELIGION* [b], Erdman, 2.

23. "Introduction" *Songs of Experience* 1, Erdman, 18.

24. *Jerusalem* 73:27, Erdman, 228.

25. *Milton* 32, Erdman, 133.

26. "If thou therefore wilt worship me, all shall be thine." Matt. 4:7.

27. In *Milton,* the great poet is moved by "A Bard's prophetic Song!" (2:22, Erdman, 96) to the realization that "The Nations still /

Follow after the detestable Gods of Priam; in pomp / Of warlike self-hood, contradicting and blaspheming,"(14[15]:14-16, Erdman, 108). The cause was his failure to cast out that Satanic voice. It is to do so that he returns, immediately, to this world (See "Miltons Track" on Pl. 32), passing through Blake to the reader, thus modeling both the rejection of the Selfhood/Satan and the sharing, the actual inter-penetration required of all who wish to join in the building of Jerusalem: "I will go down to self annihilation and eternal death, / Lest the Last Judgment come & find me unannihilate / And I be siez'd & giv'n into the hands of my own Selfhood. /.../ I in my Selfhood am that Satan: I am that Evil One!" (14[15]:22-24; 30, Erdman, 108).

28. *A Vision of The Last Judgment,* [Notebook, 85], Erdman, 563.

29. "My Spectre around me" 53-56, Erdman, 477.

30. *A Vision of the Last Judgment,* Erdman 565 [Punctuation mine].

31. *Jerusalem* 98:28-32, Erdman, 257-8.

32. *Jerusalem* 10:21, Erdman, 153.

33. *Milton* 42[49]:36-43[50]:1, Erdman, 144.

34. *Jerusalem* 27: 77-88, Erdman 173; [Italics mine].

35. Letter to Trusler, 23 Aug. 1799, Erdman, 702.

36. *Songs of Innocence,* Erdman, 7 [Italics mine].

37. *Songs of Experience,* 30:1 & 16, Erdman, 18 [Italics mine].

38. *Milton* 2:25, Erdman, 96 & see also 3:5; 4:20; 7:16 & 48; 9:7; 12:31. Is there a reader who can ignore the force of those pronouns – *my* words; *your* salvation?

39. *Jerusalem* 3, Erdman, 146 [Italics mine]. And see Jerome McGann, *The Literature of Knowledge,* p. 12, where he remarks: "Blake did not *begin* his last epic work as a broken text, he *finished* it that way." In other words, he deliberately left the opening address of his only fully illuminated version of *Jerusalem* in a state that single vision must call "mutilated," but readers who are attuned to the sensation of this mutilation will derive a powerful "meaning" in this, not least an awareness of the source of said mutilation!

40. *Jerusalem* 77, Erdman, 231 [Italics mine].

41. —— 232.

42. As quoted by Lewis Hyde, in *Trickster makes This World,* Farrar, Straus and Giroux: New York, 1998, 128.

43. What Picasso "found" was, of course, not simply what was *materially* present. In the portrait of Gertrude Stein, for instance, he famously responded to her criticism that it didn't look anything like her, "Don't worry. It will." Blake would understand perfectly.

44. That the Four exist in each of us, and that we cannot reclaim – or balance – them alone is made explicit in his manuscript poem in words often noted, but rarely considered: "Four Mighty Ones are in every Man; / a Perfect Unity / Cannot Exist. but from the Universal /Brotherhood of Eden" The Four Zoas, 1:5, Erdman, 300.

45. G.E. Bentley, Jr., *Blake Books Supplement,* Clarendon Press: Oxford 1995, 11-12.

46. Martín's remarks and his recounting of the *Popul Vuh* were recorded in Maine in June of 1996 at Robert Bly's 22nd Annual Conference on the Great Mother and the New Father.

47. The use Blake makes of the metaphor of the Printing Press should give us pause: "...here he lays his words in order above the mortal brain / As cogs are formd in a wheel to turn the cogs of the adverse wheel." *Milton* 27 [29]:9-10, Erdman, 124.

48. Descriptive Catalog, Erdman, 544.

49. *Jerusalem,* 77:22-3, Erdman, 232. The task of the Christian, that is, the artist, is spelled out in detail in the following lines (24-35); it is to heal, and pity and teach. James Elkin remarks on the specifically redemptive nature of art and the difficulty we face talking about it: "...it begins to appear that the studio work – the labor – is really about redemption. In my experience it is rarely apposite to talk directly with an artist about the underlying spiritual meaning of his or her work.... The buried spiritual content of modern and postmodern art may be the great unexplored subject in contemporary art history." *What Painting Is,* 75. Blake knew who the enemies of art were; he also knew their power.

50. "Annot. Swedenborg," *Heaven and Hell,* (London, 1784), Erdman, 601.

51. "The form of the *Marriage* is Blake's invention, and still a unique one in literature." Harold Bloom, *Commentary,* Erdman, 896.

52. Ibid.

53. *The Marriage of Heaven and Hell,* "The Argument" Erdman, 33.

54. Without belaboring the point, plates 3-8 attack Swedenborg and Milton principally for their efforts to reduce the dynamic tension in life to the categories of logic and reductive analysis. See, in this context, Blake's remark to Crabb Robinson that "Swedenborg was wrong in endeavoring to explain to the *rational* faculty what the reason cannot comprehend" Bentley, *Blake Records,* 312. Swedenborg, of course, was no poet – and so was prevented from being "of the Devils party without knowing it" (*The Marriage of Heaven and Hell,* 6, Erdman, 35).

55. *Milton* 1, Erdman, 95.

56. Public Address, [Notebook, 62], Erdman, 576.

57. *A Vision of The Last Judgment,* [Notebook 82-3], Erdman, 560.

58. "The great and golden rule of art, as well as of life, is this: That the more distinct, sharp, and wiry the bounding line, the more perfect the work of art...The want of this determinate and bounding form evidences the want of idea in the artist's mind..." Descriptive Catalogue 63-4, Erdman, 549-50.

59. "Annot. Reynolds," [Erdman, 642].

60. In *A Vision of The Last Judgment,* (Erdman, 559), Blake remarks on the distinction in passing, while describing a detail in the picture: "Multitudes are seen ascending from the Green fields of the blessed in which a Gothic Church is representative of true Art Calld Gothic in All Ages by those who follow the Fashion as that is calld which is without Shape or Fashion" This, somewhat awkward and hasty, remark may be translated as follows: The Gothic Church in my painting represents True Art, which, in all ages is labeled "Gothic" or "lacking in formal beauty and order" by those who follow the abstract fashion of thought. In another place he remarks on their horror at the spiritual nature of art, which they (naturally) label superstition. "Superstition has been long a bug bear by reason of its being united with hypocrisy, but let them be fairly seperated & then superstition will be honest feeling & God who loves all honest men will lead the poor enthusiast in the paths of holiness" "Annot. Lavater," Erdman, 598.

61. *On Homers Poetry [and] On Virgil* as reproduced in David Erdman, ed. *The Illuminated Blake,* Dover: New York, 1974, 380.

62. Where, for instance, Reynolds wrote, "...you cannot do better than have recourse to nature herself, who is always at hand," Blake responds: "Nonsense – Every Eye sees differently As the Eye – Such the Object" "Annot. to *Reynolds,*" Discourse II, [Erdman, 645]. (See also, *passim,* the Letter of August 26, 1799, to Dr. Trusler [Erdman, 702-3].

It is in this light that one must understand his remarks on Wordsworth to Crabb Robinson: "Of Wordsworth he talked as before – Some of his writings proceed from the Holy Ghost, but then others are the work of the Devil" Henry Crabb Robinson, quoted in Bentley, *Blake Records*, 321. In other words, when he is guided by Divine Imagination, Wordsworth is sublimely inspired – but when he attributes to the natural world a separate Divinity, he commits the Devil's error of idolatry, or, in modern psychological terms, " Ego projection."

63. *Public Address* [Notebook, 67], Erdman, 577.

64. *A Descriptive Catalogue*, Erdman, 541-2 [Italics added].

65. Thus Martín Prechtel, speaking before a concert of gypsy flamenco music, speaks for what Blake would call all true artists when he says: "I am not entertaining you, you know. I am giving you a gift. If you don't know what to do with it, have the courtesy to be quiet and listen. In time, you *will.*"

66. See, for example, "The Tyger," in *Songs of Experience*, Erdman, 24 and *The Marriage of Heaven and Hell*, Pl. 4: "Energy is the only life and is from the Body and Reason is the bound or outward circumference of Energy. Energy is Eternal Delight" Erdman, 34.

67. Ackroyd, *Blake: A Biography*, 338.

68. H. Crabb Robinson, quoted in *Blake Records*, 317.

69. Blake couldn't say it any more economically and clearly than Harold Stahmer, "Assuming that all speculation takes place within the limitations of language, is it not important to consider especially those speculations whose foundations are built upon a reverence and awe for language rather than upon a kind of intellectual *chutzbah* which assumes at a crucial juncture, and then falsely, that thought precedes speech, rather than vice versa." H. Stahmer in *Speak That I May See Thee! The Religious Significance of Language.* New York: Macmillan,1968, 62.

70. Dylan Thomas, "On Poetry" in *Quite Early One Morning*, New Directions, New York, 1954, 169.

71. *Laocoön*, Erdman, 274.

72. "Auguries of Innocence," Erdman, 490.

THREE: THAT IMMORTAL SOUND

1. J.T. Smith, *Nollekens and His Times,* 1828 quoted in *Blake Records,* 475.

2. See *Blake Records,* 341-2; 346-7; 349; 475; 502 & 528.

3. Blake quoted by H.C. Robinson, in *Blake Records,* 337. Gilchrist must have remembered this for, in his account of Mrs. Blake's passing, he remarks that she called to him during her dying moments, "as if he were only in the next room, to say she was coming to him, and would not be long now." Quoted in *Blake Records,* 410.

4. —— 13.

5. —— 26.

6. —— 457. None of these transcriptions has come down to us.

7. —— 305.

8. —— 482.

9. Alexander Gilchrist, *Life of William Blake 'Pictor Ignotus,'* (1863), 167.

10. I don't think it is an accident that we call this "learning by heart."

11. *The Book of Thel* I.8-11 Erdman, 3. The first time Melissa Krieger read *Thel,* before she made the effort to bring her response into words, she discovered she was weeping. Rather than try to "understand" her tears, though, she simply let them flow – and with their flowing came the flowering alluded to in the motto. Read *Thel* again; then read *Job* 28:12-15.

12. See *ALL RELIGIONS are ONE,* esp. "The Argument" and the last line: "The true Man is the source he being the Poetic Genius" Erdman, 1-2.

13. "Mark well my words! they are of your eternal salvation" *Milton* 2:25, Erdman, 96.

14. After a concert at La Scala in February of 1995, as Mr. Jarrett tells it, a member of the audience told him that the concert he had just given was, "the strongest, most moving (again putting his hand to his heart and with tears in his eyes) musical experience he had ever had, even though he had heard countless concerts at La Scala and even though he had all my recordings. My wife and I looked at each other, not really knowing what to do or say. I thanked him, but there was no proper way to say thank you for reinforcing the fragile (and at times distant) knowledge that music is in the making of the music. The heart is where the music is." Keith Jarrett, notes to the compact disc, *La Scala* ECM Records [ECM 1640] (1997). 'But,' you might argue like one of my earlier readers, 'isn't Jarrett's music recorded – and aren't Blake's finished pages also recorded, and so kept permanently – and perfectly – forever?' No. Ask any musician. When the heart stops, so does the music. What the recordings (and Blake's surviving works) show is the *possibility* of music and truth, not *the* truth or *the* music.

15. Oothoon's antagonist, Theotormon, according to Harold Bloom, "is evidently tormented by his conception of God, hence his name." Erdman, 900.

16. *VISIONS of the Daughters of Albion* 2:30-34, Erdman, 47.

17. Walter Lowrie, "'Existence' as Understood by Kierkegaard and/or Sartre," *The Sewanee Review* (July 1950) I changed Lowrie's pronouns to make the quotation better fit with Oothoon.

18. *Milton* 42[49]: 24-8 [Italics mine] Erdman, 143.

19. Notebook, 86 & 90, Erdman, 564. His echo of Matt 7:20 ("Wherefore by their fruits ye shall know them.") is deliberate and clearly implies that Christ is the source, and artists the Apostles, of art.

20. *Annotat. Lavater,* 88 Erdman, 601 [Spelling & punctuation mine]. See also Jerome J. McGann, who notes that Blake saw clearly that, "art is a set of actions carried out in the world. It is not disinterested and it is not occupied by 'virtual' space or 'virtual' realities." See *Towards a Literature of Knowledge,* (Chicago: Univ. of Chicago Press, 1989), 3-4 and also 10-16.

21. When we visit a fine museum, if we experience genuine fatigue after some hours of looking at the work, it is because we have been, ourselves, working, participating in the art, not consuming it. On the other hand, if our experience is that of dull exhaustion mixed with boredom, we have probably been either failing in our obligation to participate in the art, or finding that kind of art which is intended as a consumer object only. In this light, it is interesting to remark that, in artistic circles there is no greater insult than the charge of "selling out."

22. *Milton* 1, Erdman, 95.

23. H.C. Robinson, in *Blake Records,* 311-12 [My punctuation &

spelling].

24. *Jerusalem* 3, Erdman, 145.

25. Morton Paley writes, in his "Introduction" to The Blake Trust facsimile of *Jerusalem* (Princeton Univ. Press, 1991) that "The only explanation for such battery upon the plate is that Blake received a rebuff from a potential buyer, one that so enraged him that he wanted to remove all traces of personal intimacy and spiritual communion with his readership" [11]. I would suggest that this is maybe the only explanation that seems logical in the context of buying and selling. There are other contexts – and, probably, other reasons.

26. Jerome McGann, *Towards a Literature of Knowledge*, (Chicago: Univ. of Chicago Press, 1989), 19.

27. Bentley, Blake Records, 229.

28. —— 454.

29. —— 425.

30. —— 431.

31. Gilchrist, *Life of William Blake 'Pictor Ignotus,'* (1863), 122.

32. —— 77.

33. Mona Wilson, *The Life of William Blake*, 1932, 64-66.

34. See note 29, chapter one.

35. Again, it is hard not to see how this is not the goal of *Songs of Innocence and of Experience, The Marriage of Heaven and Hell* or, for that matter, the very first work in illuminated printing, *ALL RELIGIONS are ONE*. But that is, perhaps, another argument.

36. F.R. Leavis, "Justifying One's Valuation of Blake," lecture given at Bristol University, 15 November, 1971 reprinted in *William Blake: Essays in Honor of Sir Geoffrey Keynes* (Oxford: Clarendon Press, 1973), 82.

37. See Peter Ackroyd's *Blake: A Biography* (New York: Alfred Knopf, 1996). His retelling of the story is on pp. 208-12. James King's *William Blake: His Life* (New York: St. Martin's Press, 1991) gives a fuller, more sympathetic narrative (131-4).

38. Letter to Trusler, Aug 23, 1799 Erdman, 702 [The erratic punctuation is Blake's].

39. Ibid.

40. —— 703.

41. Ibid. The Bible, for Blake, is not primarily the recondite account of God's relations with his people, it is vision informed by the Imagination (or the Holy Spirit) and needs to be read in light of Matt. 18:3. As he put it in another place: "Jesus supposes every Thing to be Evident to the Child & to the Poor & Unlearned Such is the Gospel The Whole Bible is filld with Imaginations & Visions from End to End & not with Moral virtues" *Annotations to Berkeley's* Siris, Erdman 664. See also Blake's refutation of Dr. Johnson's remark that "the Bible is the most difficult book in the world to comprehend" (quoted in Thornton's *The Lord's Prayer, Newly Translated*): "The Beauty of the Bible is that the most Ignorant & Simple Minds Understand it Best" *Annotations to Thornton,* Erdman, 667.

42. I mean that sensation of significance which is quickly supplanted by a kind of wordless frustration as the intellect seeks to reduce what has been felt to the more familiar contours of ordinary speech. As we 'mature,' we come to believe that only that which can be made clear in direct speech is 'real.' It is the earlier experience which the paradoxes of Jesus' parables or the koans of Buddhist teachers address and seek to reclaim. In the Old Testament there are many references to this state of mind among the prophets. That recorded in Daniel will do as well as any. Here the King, Nebuchadnezzar, calls together the wise men with his dilemma: "I have dreamed a dream, and my spirit was troubled to know the dream" (Dan. 2:3). Notice that the spirit 'was troubled,' and, further, the desire for knowing (its significance) is frustrated. Then the king presents the wisemen and interpreters with the same task Blake's prophecies present: for they ask to know *what the dream was,* so that they can interpret it (according to their skill and experience). But the king replies: "The thing is gone from me: if ye will not make known unto me the dream, with the interpretation thereof, ye shall be cut in pieces, and your houses shall be made a dunghill" (Dan. 2:5). In other words, the task is not one of translation or the application of established rules; it is the complete recreation of the original visionary experience, with the interpretation appended to it. Daniel, of course, is an artist, not a critic; the task of recreation of the thing that is 'gone' is his everyday task – and with it comes, naturally, *that day's* interpretation. Those who deny the significance of Blake's great prophecies insist that in the absence of (a coherent) dream or image, their interpretations (hence ALL interpretations) must fail. It isn't coincidental that those who deny significance to Blake are likely to extend the same (dis)courtesy to Daniel. But, for a moment, take both prophets seriously: understand that your task is to both make known the dream (to the conscious mind) and the interpretation thereof. Then you'll be elucidating the text, not simply 'glossing' or reducing it to the limitations of temporal common sense.

43. In the world of time/space, Blake argues that there are but three ways by which man may glimpse reality or truth: poetry, music & painting. All three of these address reason, 'but mediately.' See *Milton* 27:55-63, Erdman, 125.

44. See *Laocoön,* note 71, chapter two.

45. *Milton* 41:2-10, Erdman, 142.

46. *A Vision of The Last Judgment* [82-3], Erdman, 560. (Slightly altered and punctuated for clarity).

47. John 10:14-15.

48. "The Verse" A note attached (along with the Arguments to the individual books) to the second edition of *Paradise Lost* by the poet. See Merritt Hughes, ed. *John Milton: Complete Poems and Major Prose,* Odyssey Press, New York, 1957, 210. That Milton's opening sentence announces "The Measure" of the poem suggests it is the source of Blake's title to his remarks: "Of the Measure…"

49. *Jerusalem* 3, Erdman, 145. Jesus' words (Matt. 28:18) were originally etched by Blake in Greek and later erased from the plate. See also Mk. 16:15-18; Lk. 24:49, and John. 21:22.

50. *Milton* 1: Preface, & 21[23]:58, Erdman, 95 & 116; See also *Jerusalem* 34[38]:17-24, Erdman, 180.

51. *Jerusalem* 91:18-21, Erdman, 251.

52. Jeremiah 5:21.

53. Public Address, [Notebook, 20], Erdman, 580-81.

54. Nelson Hilton remarks that he believes much of the difficulty in Blake Criticism is owing to the fact that we don't yet have "an adequate metalanguage" for dealing with his texts. Amen! I say, nor are we ever likely to manage this metalanguage so long as we assume that what Blake looks for in his readers is no more than thinking and writing about him! What he requires is what any prophet requires, not a meta-discourse, but a changed life. Specifically that we sing and dance with him into Jerusalem. See Nelson Hilton, "Reading Blake, Blake

Reading" *New Orleans Review* Vol. XIII, No. 3 (Fall, 1986), 39.

55. *Jerusalem* 53:1, Erdman, 202.

56. —— 3, Erdman, 145-6.

57. I can't resist pointing out to my students that the word tells us what the artist does: he or she *per-forms;* gives form to the truth of the moment. Yeats knew this too; somewhere he remarks that poems can evoke the truth but never contain it.

58. One of my early readers, Tom Devine, remarked that this doesn't follow logically. "*You,*" he wrote, "are now a part of the meaning of W.B. for *me,* but how am I (as a reader) part of it for you?" What lies beneath this question is a generally shared notion that the writer cannot be truly connected to his reader because they may be separated by unbridgable distances and impossible spans of time. But is the tree, grown from the seed carried across the ocean in the belly of a bird, not joined by the seed to the original in ways unknown to both – and are not both trees changed by the circumstances of the voyage and the different soils and climate? I know this is a metaphor in which the reader is alternately soil and a tree and that the mind wants them separate and separable, wants the tree to be more important than the seed and the seed more important than the soil – but all that wanting doesn't change anything in reality: we live in the moment – and the moment connects us to Eternity. Always. I think this may be the way out of the misery of 'identity politics.' For this notion, that our importance comes in some way from what we share with others in the tribe – language, skin color, gender, DNA – imagines that communities are made of similarities. Blake knows better. Jerusalem and her builders are the only community. And they are individuals joined in and by Eternity, not cogs in a wheel. Blake says, remember: "Opposition is true friendship." Thanks, Tom.

59. Of course, Blake wouldn't agree that because meaning is unstable in this time/space universe, there is no stable meaning. Paradox is always at the root of profoundly spiritual and artistic work. And that is precisely what Blake calls us to: spiritual work on which our salvation rests.

60. "Mathematic Form is Eternal in the Reasoning Memory. Living Form is Eternal Existence. Grecian is Mathematic Form [.] Gothic is Living Form" *On Virgil,* Erdman, 270.

61. Suppose that when we limit poetry to marks on a page and to scansion schemes based on classical prosody we think of ourselves as limiting or fettering it? Suddenly a whole series of meanings opens up for several of Blake's interesting remarks about poetry and the human spirit: to begin with, in his remarks "On the Measure" of *Jerusalem:* "Poetry Fetter'd, Fetters the Human Race!" (Erdman, 146) suggests that so long as his poem is confined to the page, the whole race suffers. Further, we find, in the Notebook the observation: "Deceit to secresy confind / Lawful, cautious & refind / To every thing but interest blind / And forges fetters for the mind" (Erdman, 472), which may have inspired some of his most famous lines, in *Songs of Experience:* "In every cry of every Man, / In every Infants cry of fear, / In every voice: in every ban, / The mind-forg'd manacles I hear" "London," Erdman, 27.

FOUR: TO BE UNDERSTOOD

1. From *The Cutting of an Agate* (quoted in *The Creative Process,* ed. B. Ghiselin: Univ. of California Press, Berkeley, 1952, 106-7).

2. That our society or culture wishes to suppress this impulse, and that our "educational systems" are so largely devoted to that suppression is a cause, I think, of Blake's unrelenting hostility to education and schools.

3. Verses in a Letter to Thomas Butts, Oct 2, 1800, Erdman, 712. See also *Jerusalem* 33[37]:17-22, Erdman, 180.

4. Reality itself might be defined as that which falls within the sound of one's voice, or, as Blake puts it in *Milton,* that space on the verges of which the sun rises and sets and which constitutes man's spatial universe (*Milton* 29[31]:4-12). That he doesn't mean by these limits as far as a man can *see* is clear in the lines that follow: "As to that false appearance which appears to the reasoner, / As of a Globe rolling through Voidness, it is a delusion of Ulro / The Microscope knows not of this nor the Telescope" (*Milton* 29[31]:15-17). For the only way to pass this limit is in thought, that is, in abstraction. Of course, one can employ abstraction to wonderful effect. Newton, for instance, by giving abstract law to the motion of bodies in space, enabled the science of artillery.

5. See *Milton* 3:28-30, Erdman, 97 and *Jerusalem* 32[36]:9, 14, 15, 19, Erdman, 178.

6. Charlie Knight, a Ute Indian, tells us: "If you know my song, you know Charlie. Everyone has a song. God gives us each a song. That's how we know who we are. Our song tells us who we are." But this song must be SUNG; it comes through the body. Tharmas patiently waits for you to sing – and until you sing, you won't really know who you are. In Kafka's famous fable, he waits by the door – and he will wait, if you make him, for your whole life. Harvy Arden and Steve Wall, *Wisdomkeepers Meetings with Native American Spiritual Elders*, Hillsboro, Oregon: Beyond Words Publishing, 1990, 16.

7. See note 35, chapter three.

8. Blake, though buried in the Dissenter's burial grounds in Bunhill Fields and though baptized and married in the Church of England, was never (save for a brief flirtation with the Swedenborgians) associated with any congregation and cannot be called a "practicing" parishioner in any sense. His religion was his art and life. See Peter Ackroyd, *Blake* (Alfred Knopf: New York, 1996), 100-104.

9. *ALL RELIGIONS are ONE, The Early Illuminated Books*, Eaves, Essick, & Viscomi, 51 & 53. I have reproduced in type the distribution of the letters on the original plates because the breaks, (Nati-ons; Spirit & vari-ous) are part of the meaning. See also *The Marriage of Heaven and Hell*, 11: "...All deities reside in the human breast." Erdman, 38; in Erdman, *ALL RELIGIONS are ONE* is on pp. 1 & 2, but without Blake's arrangement of letters.

10. As F.R. Leavis put it. See note 36, chapter three.

11. And see note 44, chapter one.

12. Though the usual term for Blake's designs is "plate," I believe "scene," which I discovered in Allan Cunningham's early essay on Blake [1830], is far better suited to Blake's art. The dynamism thus accorded to the design is a powerful warning to us that the world of imagination is not simply a *textual* one. Some pages later Cunningham also supplies a suggestive term for the Job engravings, referring to them as "The Inventions for the Book of Job." See *Blake Records*, 483 and 499.

13. Blake's intended audience, as is I hope clear by now, is not primarily a reading one. Therefore, as much as possible, I have substituted "audience" for "reader." There are even stronger reasons for the use of "audience" as will be clear later on.

14. I am struck by the irony of the fact that those works illuminated by Blake's own hand have ended up in the possession of academies and immensely wealthy private persons, precisely the people he found most contemptible. Was this, then, what he intended with his process? To make, through the laws of scarcity, his work into a medium of cash exchange?! Both the works and the life say otherwise.

15. One side benefit of this exercise is that it "weeds out" the class very effectively. It is fun for me to listen to the various reasons given me as I sign the drop slips that come in during the week, but, more importantly, it helps to narrow the class right away to those who are intrigued – and willing to give it a try.

16. "There is a place where Contrarieties are equally True / This place is called Beulah, It is a pleasant lovely Shadow / Where no dispute can come." *Milton* 30[33]:1-3, Erdman, 129.

17. And to supplement it, I also use a "singing bowl"; a tuned brass bowl which is made to vibrate by circling the outer edge of it with a roughened wand. The sound produced is powerful and seems to come from all directions. Students enjoy both performing on the bowl – and seeing it as a symbol of exactly what Blake intends: the bowl is the circle of Blake's audience; the wand is the performance of the poem; and the sound is the reality of Fourfold vision.

18. Some critics are made uneasy by this; according to Peter Ackroyd, for instance, she took her lead from her husband, following his example rather than employing her own intuition or inspiration. Not only was she reduced, that is, to a mechanical copyist, "it is even possible for scholars to determine which were colored by her and which by her husband" (184). I'm sure *they* believe they know this. But I am not convinced they know what they are talking about. See Ackroyd, *Blake* (Alfred Knopf: New York, 1996), 119, 183-4, 186, 220, 224 & 355.

19. Hayley's letter of July 15, 1802 to Lady Hesketh, quoted in Bentley, *Blake Records,* 106.

20. Quoted in Bently, *Blake Records,* 482.

21. W.B. Yeats, *Plays and Controversies.* Macmillan: New York, 1924,

173.

22. —— 176 [Italics mine].

23. —— 177.

24. Quoted by Mona Wilson, in *The Life of William Blake,* 1932, 278.

25. "Annot. Berkeley's *Siris,*" Erdman, 664.

26. "...less than All cannot satisfy Man." *THERE is NO NATURAL RELIGION,* Erdman, 2. "Error is Created Truth is Eternal" *A Vision of The Last Judgment,* Erdman, 565. That eternal truth is the "all" we thirst for – and it is the error in our creations which we mourn when we see them, as we say, "in the light of day."

27. "On Homers Poetry," Erdman, 269.

28. "The Four Zoas," 1.12, Erdman, 301.

29. This is true, and Blake understood it to be so, not only for music, but for painting, poetry – and architecture (by which four he represented all the arts [See *Milton* 27:55-64, Erdman, 125 & the *Laocoön,* Erdman, 274]). It is that sense of the music, which must be present in every part as well as the whole, which makes the poet throw out even beautiful lines and striking metaphors when they are false or 'out of tune;' the painter, the dancer, the actor, the architect – all report the same experience.

30. Blake identifies Tharmas, the Zoa of Touch or Sensation, with the Tongue; see *Jerusalem* 12:60, Erdman, 186 and 14:4, Erdman, 158.

31. Most famously, in the openings of *Songs of Innocence:* "Sing thy songs of happy chear" and *Songs of Experience:* "Hear the voice of the Bard!" Erdman, 7 & 18.

32. *Jerusalem* 3:1-10, Erdman, 145.

33. "I believe both Macpherson & Chatterton, that what they say is Ancient, Is so" and "I own myself an admirer of Ossian equally with any other Poet whatever" Annotations to Wordsworth's *Poems,* Erdman, 665-6.

34. "The Learned, who strive to ascend into Heaven by means of learning, appear to Children like dead horses" is the subject, borrowed from Swedenborg, of one of Blake's visionary paintings (See Descriptive Catalogue, #VIII, Erdman, 546) But Blake also told Crabb Robinson that "...Swedenborg was wrong in endeavouring to explain to the *rational* faculty what the reason cannot comprehend" Quoted in

Bentley, *Blake Records* 312. See note 53, chapter two.

35. *Milton* 13[14]:49-14[15]:3, Erdman, 107-8.

36. Ferdinand Ebner, *Cf. Ferdinand Ebner Schriften.* ed. F. Seyr [Munchen: Kosel Verlag, 1963-64] Vol. 1, 417 (quoted by H. Stahmer in *Speak That I May See Thee! The Religious Significance of Language.* New York: Macmillan, 1968, 237).

37. "Introduction" *Songs of Experience,* Erdman, 18 & John. 1:3.

38. Ps. 19:2-5; 14. To get an even stronger sense of the power of the sung word, see David Rosenberg's modern translation in *A Poet's Bible* (Hyperion: New York, 1991), 11-15.

39. *Milton* 6:26, Erdman, 100.

40. —— 22[24]:15-21, Erdman, 117.

41. *Jerusalem* 27:17-20, Erdman, 172.

42. Mk. 12:1.

43. I am indebted to James Elkins for pointing out that Alchemists, "never tired of pointing out that *labor* [struggle] and *ora* [prayer] spell laboratory." Art is struggle. It is work. And it is prayer. See *What Painting Is,* 37.

44. See the distinction between Allegory and Vision in the opening of *A Vision of The Last Judgment,* Erdman, 554.

45. *Public Address,* Erdman, 578.

46. *The Marriage of Heaven and Hell* 10:9, Erdman, 38.

47. Christopher Middleton, quoted by August Kleinzahler in a review of his book, *Intimate Chronicles,* (Sheep Meadow Press, 1966) in the *Three Penny Review* No. 72, Winter 1997, 11.

48. Terri Banks, personal journal February 19, 1997.

49. W.B. Yeats, "A Prayer for Old Age" *Poems of W.B. Yeats,* ed. Finneran, New York: Macmillan, 1983, 282.

50. Melissa Krieger, personal journal, February 23, 1997.

51. Susan Rudolph, personal journal, February 20, 1997.

52. "Disruption, Hesitation, Silence" in *Proofs & Theories. Essays on Poetry* (Hopewell, N.J.: The Ecco Press, 1994), 73.

53. G.M. Hopkins makes this point in "As kingfishers catch fire;" the relevant lines as follows: Each mortal thing does one thing and the same: / Deals out that being indoors each one dwells; / Selves – goes its self; *myself* it speaks and spells, / Crying *What I do is me: for that I came.*"

54. "Descriptive Catalogue [63-4], Erdman, 549-50.

55. In Great Eternity, every particular Form gives forth or Emanates / Its own peculiar Light, & the Form is the Divine Vision / And the Light is his Garment This is Jerusalem in every Man / A Tent & Tabernacle of Mutual Forgiveness Male & Female / Clothings. / And Jerusalem is called Liberty among the Children of Albion *Jerusalem* 54:1-5, Erdman, 203.

56.

> For Mercy has a human heart
> Pity, a human face:
> And Love, the human form divine,
> And Peace, the human dress.
>
> Then every man in every clime,
> That prays in his distress,
> Prays to the human form divine
> Love Mercy Pity Peace.
>
> And all must love the human form,
> In heathen, turk or jew.
> Where Mercy, Love & Pity dwell,
> There God is dwelling too

"The Divine Image" in *Songs of Innocence* Erdman, 13. This Song is sometimes placed in *Experience*, between "The Ecchoing Green" & "The Chimney Sweep."

POSTLUDE: A MEMORABLE FANCY

1. Liner notes to the compact disc recording, Rykodisc [red-103939] (1997).

Acknowledgments

You wouldn't be reading this if Norm Minnick & Chris Jansen hadn't insisted on my getting it published and Norm agreeing to edit it. And it would not have ever come to be written were it not for the contributions of the students in a series of courses I offered in Blake over the years. It was they who made the building of Jerusalem after the example of the poet collectively possible and without them there would be no book at all. Here are their names: Deborah Marie Agard, Timothy Paul Ayers, Terri Banks, Jeffrey Wayne Beck, Emily Bick, Barbara Bishop, Catherine Ridder Bohannon, Andy Alexander Blythe, Allison Lee Bush, Matthew Sander Carlson, Chelsea Casperson, Sara Casperson, Kristin D. Chapman, Tyler Anthony Cook, Jodi E. Cornacchione, Colleen Ann Fearrin, Jeffrey Michael Flannagan, Daniel Fox, Kristen Marie Frank, Sarah Jean Gardner, Laura Michelle Goodenow, John Wesley Gosney, Mindy Gutowski, Kevin Michael Halm, Christina Susanne Hasty, Jacqueline Ardath Hawk, Cheryl Janine Hazelwood, Marjorie Heckel, Julia M. Heller, David Edward Hoffman, Karli Hilton, Ruth D. Hubbard, Robin Hurley, Keith Huser, Jillian John, Kim Jones, John Koprowski, Mari Koslowski, Melissa Krieger, Kimberly Ann Kutska, Shuhong Krott, Maya Ann Lagu, David Franklin Lary, Brad Latino, Leticia Corinne Liggett, Jessica Elizabeth Lollino, Geoffrey Lord, Eric Macy, Matthew Wayne Marietta, Deborah Leah McKee, Kevin Maupin, Andrew Jacob Meier, Erin Shea Metcalf, Evan Michner, Jackie Ann Miller, Michael Lee Millington, Minka Aranka Misangyi, Jennifer Ann Mullen, Theresa Gail Murphy, Dani Nier-Weber, Richard Scott Nokes, Carolyn Oravecz, Paul Jacob Patterson, Jennifer Price, Alisa Pykett, Tony Reed, Heather Sarah Ross, Susan Rudolph, Nina Ryan, Catherine Julia Sahuc, Tak Sato, Megan Schildmier, Jennifer Lynn Seward, Kelly D. Shaw, Peter Michael Evan Sheldon, Jennie Ann Snider, Jennifer Leigh Stiles, Theodore Stone, Carol Stumpf, Eliza Alice Tudor, Marie Ann Ursuy, Jessica Leah Wills, James Joseph Zeigler. To each and every one of these I am eternally in debt. And, along with the students I must also remember to thank the Angels who visited the classes and shared so graciously their special gifts – dancing, singing, painting, song-writing and performing, and soul-opening. The first, Fran Quinn, was with us from the very beginning (Spring of '92) and taught us stumbling readers how to find the tempo in Blake's verse and was always available to help us read and sing Blake's Prophetic Books. Next was Ann Igoe who came from South Carolina in February of '97 (and returned in '99!) to teach us how to understand the body language of Blake's visionary personae and how to discover Blake in the very movement of our bodies! She also read – and made many useful suggestions for – the first draft of this book. In 2001, Martín Prechtel, author, performer, shaman and extraordinary spell-binder came to show us how to grasp the way Blake's extraordinary combination of color and design, word and sound lift us out of clock-time and empty space. From the first chord on his guitar to the long and charged silence three hours later, we were all moving easily in eternity with William. In that same class, in 2001, Nina Ryan turned up. An Indianapolis performance artist and dancer, she took up Ann Igoe's baton and volunteered to help me teach the embodiment of Blake! And then she returned in '05 on her own time to take the class again and again help us leave our self-consciousness at the door and carry our real bodies into the future. And in that same year – the last time I offered the class – we were also joined by Judith-Kate Friedman, who not only sang Blake with us, but taught us how to write and sing our own, collective song! I can never thank these angels enough; each of them agreed without hesitation, to take on the terrific challenge of responding to Blake's art and sharing their special insights with us. They, too, were builders of Jerusalem. I would also like to thank two eminent Blakean scholars, Tristanne Connolly and Alicia Ostriker, for their kind words and encouragement. And finally, without the opportunity to try out my ideas on my wife, Lee Verner, and without her feedback and suggestions I would never have dared to offer the course, let alone write the book.

ABOUT THE AUTHOR

Jim Watt was born in Los Angeles and grew up in Southern Oregon in and around Grants Pass. After graduating from High School, he joined the Marines to see the world, which turned out to consist of Southern California and Japan. After completing his tour of duty (1958-1962), he avoided the mundane work world by using the G.I. Bill to earn a B.A. (1967) at Portland (Oregon) State College and an M.A. (1969) and Ph.D. (1977) at the University of North Carolina at Chapel Hill. From 1970 until 2007, he was an English professor at Butler University in Indianapolis, Indiana. He taught literature and writing as well as courses in the History of Science, the Gothic Cathedral and playwriting among other odd subjects. Three of his full-length dramas were produced in Indianapolis: *Taken Literally*, a comedy at the Broad Ripple Theatre Original Works Festival in 1989; *Sour Noodles: A Koan for Americans* at the Phoenix Theatre New Works Series in 1984; and *Help From a Man*, a drama for the Indianapolis Civic Theatre's Indiana Playwright's Project in 1990. In 1992, he offered a Seminar in the Prophetic Poetry of William Blake, about which he knew almost nothing despite having written a Master's Thesis on Blake's poem *Milton*, a radical re-vision of *Paradise Lost*. The experience of finding a way into Blake along with his students was so profound, he offered the seminar five more times between 1995 and 2005. *Work Toward Knowing* is his effort to capture the perils and joys of this on-going adventure.

COLOPHON

This book was edited and designed by
Norman Minnick.

The text face is Baskerville, designed in 1754 by
John Baskerville (1706-1775).

Baskerville's refined design marks a point of transition
between 'old' faces like William Caslon's, with a
heritage going back to the fifteenth century,
and 'modern' faces like the designs of
Giambattista Bodoni and
Firmin Didot.

CPSIA information can be obtained at www.ICGtesting.com
Printed in the USA
LVOW11s0416230316

480353LV00001B/9/P

9 781312 990401